UNDERSTANDING
DEPRESSION

UNDERSTANDING DEPRESSION

A Complete Guide to Its Diagnosis and Treatment

Donald F. Klein, M.D.
Paul H. Wender, M.D.

OXFORD
UNIVERSITY PRESS

2005

OXFORD

UNIVERSITY PRESS

Oxford University Press, Inc., publishes works that further
Oxford University's objective of excellence
in research, scholarship, and education.

Oxford   New York
Auckland   Cape Town   Dar es Salaam   Hong Kong   Karachi
Kuala Lumpur   Madrid   Melbourne   Mexico City   Nairobi
New Delhi   Shanghai   Taipei   Toronto

With offices in
Argentina   Austria   Brazil   Chile   Czech Republic   France   Greece
Guatemala   Hungary   Italy   Japan   Poland   Portugal   Singapore
South Korea   Switzerland   Thailand   Turkey   Ukraine   Vietnam

Published by Oxford University Press, Inc.
198 Madison Avenue, New York, New York 10016
www.oup.com

First published in 1993 by Oxford University Press, Inc.

First issued as an Oxford University Press paperback, 1994

Oxford is a registered trademark of Oxford University Press

Library of Congress Cataloging-in-Publication Data
Klein, Donald F., 1928-
Understanding depression : a complete guide to its diagnosis and
treatment / Donald F. Klein, Paul H. Wender.— Rev. and expanded ed.
p. cm.
Includes index.
ISBN-13: 978-0-19-515614-0 (paper)—ISBN-13: 978-0-19-515613-3 (cloth)
ISBN-10: 0-19-515614-5 (paper)—ISBN-10: 0-19-515613-7 (cloth)
1. Depression, Mental—Popular works.
I. Wender, Paul H., 1934-
II. Title.
RC537.K543 2005
616.85'27—dc22
2004016079

1 3 5 7 9 8 6 4 2

Printed in the United States of America
on acid-free paper

To our patients from whom we have learned much, and to sufferers of depression and bipolar disorder in the hope that this book helps them to cope with their disease.

Why We Wrote This Book

As psychiatrists who have been involved in research with psychiatric patients for almost 30 years, we have been increasingly impressed by the evidence that many severe psychiatric disorders are diseases. They are often hereditary, arising from physiological malfunctions (especially in brain chemistry), and their symptoms can be lessened or eliminated by treatment with medication. We have been particularly interested in measuring the effectiveness of drug treatment, a task that involves comparisons with other treatments, including psychological therapies. This field of research is a rapidly growing one. A striking gap has grown between what is known by clinicians and researchers and what is known by the public, even the psychologically sophisticated public. Because depressive illness, which can be devastating to individuals and their families, affects a large part of the population and does respond well to drug treatment, we think it is important to bring to the general public the most recent information on the research findings in this area.

Because of the knowledge gap, the majority of people with serious depression—most often biological depression—either receive no treatment at all or receive inappropriate treatment. The public has been subjected to a bewildering flood of books explaining the origins of unhappiness—including depression—and other forms of human misery. Most of these books have one thing in common: the positions they advance are not supported by scientific data. The information provided here differs in that it is supported by hard evidence that is now common knowledge among an increasingly large group of psychiatric specialists.

One of the important components in the treatment of biological depression is education about its causes, symptoms, treatment, and outcome, and the special problems associated with it. Because it frequently is a chronic disease, the most effective treatment requires that the patient and the family be well educated about the patient's illness. This book is, in essence, a written version of the "course" we give to the depressed patients we treat. It is a product of what we have learned, including what our patients have taught us.

Why We Wrote a Second Edition

Since the publication of the first edition of the book in 1993, new medications for the treatment of depression have been developed and studies have been conducted evaluating the effectiveness of treatment with medication and psychotherapies. It is the purpose of this second edition to discuss these new treatments. Also, we will discuss difficulties that stand in the way of discovering and evaluating new treatments.

Contents

UNDERSTANDING
DEPRESSION

1

Introduction

DEPRESSION MAY be a normal human emotion—a response to loss, disappointment, or failure. Some depressions, however, should more properly be put in the category of common biological *diseases*, destructive to families, to careers, to relationships. Depression can be lethal. It has been estimated that perhaps somewhere between 10 and 30 percent of depressives and manic-depressives kill themselves. But the figure may actually be lower; obtaining exact figures is extremely difficult. What is known is that since the widespread use of the "selective serotonin reuptake inhibitors" (SSRIs) such as Prozac, suicide rates have declined substantially in a number of countries.

If you have picked up this book and are reading this sentence, there is a good chance that you are worried about depression in yourself or others in your family. Most serious depression requires medical treatment even through it may be triggered or worsened by psychological factors. Correct medical diagnosis should lead to a treatment that in most instances is effective, moderately fast, and inexpensive.

The aims of this book are:

1. To explain what biological depression is and to clarify the difference between depression, a normal emotion, and biological depression, and illness.

2. To give the reader brief self-screening tests that can help to determine if he or she (or a relative or friend) requires further evaluation.

3. To describe other psychiatric disorders that are associated with biological depression, such as manic-depression and panic attacks.

4. To indicate how someone suffering from biological depression can find help.

5. To provide *a family guide* to the treatment of biological depression and related disorders.

6. To discuss in some detail the treatment of depression.

7. To discuss problems in the development of new treatments and improving medical care.

Let us elaborate on these points:

1. Biological depression is common—in fact, depression and manic-depression are among the most common physical disorders seen in psychiatry. One woman in five and one man in ten can expect to develop a depression or manic-depression sometime during the course of their lives. In other words, one person in seven can expect to develop depression or manic-depression during his or her lifetime—in total, well over 30 million of the current United States population.

Untreated depressive illness can lead to personal, familial, and social disasters. A particularly vivid statement of what it means to be severely depressed comes from Russell Hampton's autobiography, *The Far Side of Despair* (1975):

If there were a physical disease that manifested itself in some particularly ugly way, such as pustulating sores or a sloughing off of the flesh accompanied by pain of an intense and chronic nature, readily visible to everyone, and if that disease affected fifteen million people in our country, and further, if there were virtually no help or succor for most of these persons, and they were forced to walk among us in their obvious agony, we would rise up as one social body in sympathy and anger. We would give of our resources, both human and economic, and we would plead and demand that this suffering be eased. There isn't such a physical disease, but there is such a disease of the mind, and about fifteen million people around us are suffering from it. But we have not risen in anger and sympathy, although they are walking among us in their pain and anguish.

Depressive illness is common, painful, and dangerous, but since Russell Hampton wrote that passage, new effective treatments for depression have been developed that yield excellent results, and we will discuss these in a moment. Yet, in spite of our progress, the number of people in the United States currently suffering from this disease is probably twice the number stated by Hampton.

With regard to the lethality of depression, suicide is the eighth leading cause of death in adults (often through apparent accidents) and is the second leading cause of death in children and adolescents. The ability to recognize depressive illness in yourself or loved ones may be a matter of life and death.

2. Our second aim, to provide a self-screening test for depression, is directed at the widespread inability to recognize depression (and therefore the failure to secure proper treatment for it).

3. Our third goal is to help the reader recognize conditions related to depression—such as mania (one phase of manic-depression) and a milder depressive disorder called *dysthymia*. The tests we provide for depression and the other conditions are like those used by psychiatrists in diagnosing these illnesses. For some related disorders, such as panic attacks, we are not providing a self-screening test but believe that our description is clear enough for easy recognition.

The purpose of these self-screening tests is not to enable you to make a diagnosis. Rather, the purpose is to help you to know when to seek expert help. People can be taught to recognize the warning symptoms of depressive illness (and panic attacks), just as they have been taught to detect the warning symptoms of cancer. The purpose of the American Cancer Society's "seven warning signs of cancer" is not to enable people to diagnose

themselves but to teach them to watch for suggestive symptoms—
for example, to examine the breast for lumps and to be alert for
sores that do not heal or moles that change color. Learning to
observe such bodily changes contributed to a medical early
warning system.

The prospective patient is in a better position to find *possible*
early signs of cancer than the doctor is. Usually such symptoms are not signs of cancer. But if they are, they will have been
detected early—and the cancer will be more likely to respond
to treatment. In the same way, we want people who read this
book to be able to recognize the early symptoms of depression.
We want to teach them a psychiatric early warning system so
that they can get treatment for themselves or someone close to
them before the danger has mounted.

People know when they are sad, of course, and understandably do not think of that feeling—and the related feeling called
depression—as an illness. Depressive illness can be insidious
because it frequently resembles the kind of unhappiness that is
a normal part of human living. Without help, most people cannot distinguish between psychological depression and biological depressive illness. One reason is that most people, when
depressed, immediately trace their emotional state to problems
in their current or past life, failing to recognize distinctive clues
hinting that they may instead be suffering from a disease. Another reason is that biological depression can be triggered by
life events, which may lead people to discount depressive disease as simply normal psychological responses.

4. It is essential that people who suspect they are suffering
from depression know who is qualified to help. Not all physicians or mental health workers—such as psychologists, social
workers, and psychiatric nurses—have had adequate training
in the diagnosis and treatment of depression. Since 1980 the
American Psychiatric Association has published a diagnostic
manual that defines the various mental disorders in concrete
language that is easy to understand. However, simply reading
descriptions of diagnoses does not provide sufficient training.
The student must also have years of expertly supervised experience in order to apply these definitions in a reliable way. The

availability of the diagnostic manual has stimulated the teaching of diagnosis across the range of mental health workers, but the best treatment of depression requires further specialization. However, while some of these other mental health workers have learned to diagnose depression, many have not and may fail to recognize these disorders. And, more important, some may treat depressive and manic-depressive patients only with counseling or psychotherapy, preventing them from getting appropriate treatment with medication.

Another problem is that nonmedical therapists cannot provide complete treatment of depression because the optimum treatment often involves the use of medication; only physicians can prescribe antidepressant medication. Those who cannot prescribe antidepressant medication sometimes tend to downplay its importance. Even some psychiatrists, however, do not have sufficient training to diagnose or treat biological depression correctly because the field is relatively new and rapidly growing.

Because biological depression is frequently chronic, it may require long-term continuing treatment, like any other chronic biological illness. This treatment is best administered by psychiatrists who specialize in biological psychiatry. There is a vast difference in the training of psychiatrists and that of family physicians or internists. The psychiatrists spend three years studying the treatment of psychiatric disease, including a substantial period learning the best techniques for administering medication. It is essential that people who suspect they are suffering from depression know whom to approach for help. It is extremely important to consult a qualified physician, usually a biological psychiatrist, in order to secure both accurate diagnosis and correct treatment.

The family practitioner may have only six months of training in psychiatry, and the internist usually has less. Though such physicians may have acquired much "clinical experience," their training has usually been *on-the-job*. Some physicians have taken special courses and expanded their clinical experience with a view to becoming expert in the treatment of depression. However, these doctors are in the minority. An extremely important development for the health of the public would be a move toward helping family practitioners to recognize the importance of depression and to include an examination for depression in their standard patient evaluation. Nevertheless, in the treatment of mental illness as in the rest of medicine, the specialist—the biological psychiatrist—is likely to be more familiar with advanced techniques. If one needs to have his thyroid gland removed, one wants to be operated on by a thyroid specialist, not by a general surgeon, whose experience is in a variety of areas and who has performed fewer such operations than the thyroid specialist.

Since both psychiatrists and family physicians may not have an adequate background to diagnose and treat biological depression, the patient must take an active, often uncomfortable role by asking the physician if he or she has had a special interest or training in depression and is widely experienced in the use of medication for this disease. It is also helpful to ask about the physician's attitude toward psychotherapy. If he indicated that psychotherapy is the core of the treatment and that medication is only a minor adjunct to be used as little as possible, he is not up-to-date.

On the other hand, the role of the psychiatrist has not been reduced to writing prescriptions. He must take the time to get to know the patient by systematic detailed inquiry and medical examinations. Furthermore, he must take the time to answer all the patient's questions about outcome, symptoms, side effects, course, relapse, prognosis, heredity, etc.—or he is not providing adequate care.

5. The most effective treatment *requires that the patient and his or her family* be active participants. The family's understanding of the patient's illness and the family's relationship to the patient can support or undercut medical treatment and can psychologically amplify or diminish symptoms. The family's roles are multiple, including "caring," monitoring the patient's symptoms, and helping the physician assess the patient's response to treatment. The views of depressives and manic-depressives of their world are altered by the distorting lenses of their illness. The family can help immensely by providing an objective view of the patient's functioning.

In urging family participation, we are not referring to "codependency"—a current faddish term in psychiatry and clinical psychology. This word refers to the (usually undocumented) notion that the patient's illness is supported, encouraged, or amplified by other family members. "Codependency" is misleading as well as faddish. Since biological depression is a disease, it can neither be caused nor cured by changes in the way the family related to the patient. The family's actions can worsen or lessen the patient's symptoms, but only to a limited extent. The family has a major impact upon helping the patient get appropriate care; if the family is misguided, it can prevent the patient from receiving such care by belittling or denying the seriousness of the illness.

6. We want next to discuss the treatment of depression. The evidence is compelling that effective medical treatment can relieve or totally remove the symptoms in over 80 percent of people with severe depression. The antidepressant medications are not habit-forming or abusable. Research studies have shown that the administration of antidepressants in normal people produces certain side effects but no "high" feelings or euphoria. In the more than 40 years that they have been available, they have never been sold on the "street" as illegal drugs. There has been much misguided and sensational discussion of antidepressant drugs in the popular press.

In urging treatment of depressive disease by medication, we are not ignoring the possible usefulness of psychotherapy. However, we believe that the prescription of antidepressant medication should almost always be the first step in the treatment of *biological* depression. Following relief of symptoms through the use of medication, psychotherapy may be able to alleviate many of the residual psychological symptoms.

This book will deal only briefly with theoretical issues that are of interest to people studying depression. We will say something about brain chemistry and its relationship to mood, but for the most part we will direct our attention to practical issues.

One last point—the most important point. This is not another self-help book. Our overriding message is that certain forms of depression *cannot* be overcome by self-help. They require medical evaluation and medical treatment. The purpose of this book is to assist people to recognize when they need professional help, to indicate how they can get that help, and to clarify how they can best work with the health provider in the treatment of the disease of biological depression. We also hope to inform our readers of problems improving their treatment.

2

Symptoms of Mood Disorders: Recognizing Biological Depression

The Question of Names

THE NAMES of the "mood disorders" have changed repeatedly, and the layperson is generally confused about their meaning. The mood disorders we will discuss are: depression or unipolar depression, manic-depression or bipolar disorder, dysthymic disorder, and cyclothymic disorder. There are two major types of depression. In the first, *depression* or *unipolar depression*, the patient's mood varies between being either normal or depressed; he or she never becomes excessively elated. In the second, *manic-depression* or *bipolar illness*, the patient's mood varies between being depressed (as in unipolar depression) and being "high" or "euphoric." In the past manic-depression was sometimes called *manic-depressive psychosis*. *Psychosis* is another word for "insanity," including symptoms such as delusions (false beliefs) and hallucinations. We now realize that most people with manic-depression are never psychotic. *Dysthymia* refers to a state of mild chronic depression. *Cyclothymia* refers to a condition in which the person's moods swing up and down for days, weeks, or months at a time, with symptoms that are not as severe as those in manic-depression.

There is also much confusion about whether these illnesses are produced by psychological experiences or by malfunctioning within the brain (a "chemical imbalance"). The major point we wish to make is that depression, manic-depression, dysthymic disorder, and cyclothymic disorder are diseases, the product of abnormal biological functioning. We will use the terms biological depression, clinical depression, and depressive illness interchangeably.

With depressive illness, as with any other disease, the physician—the psychiatrist—has guidelines and rules for making the diagnosis. The rules used for diagnosing depressive illness are simple. They depend on the presence or absence of symptoms that anyone can recognize. The layperson can use these rules to rate himself and come to a rough conclusion:

I probably do have a depressive illness.
I might have a depressive illness.
I don't have a depressive illness.

The words "might" and "probably" are used because determining how severe a symptom is—or isn't—is a "judgment call." The skilled psychiatrist's expertise involves the ability to judge the seriousness of a person's symptoms. This judgment is based on experience with many patients and includes the ability to judge not only what a person says but how he says it. The psychiatrist uses a systematic interview to evaluate what a depressed person tells him. This can be used to fill out a comprehensive rating scale and is more accurate than giving people questionnaires.

Here we present the psychiatrist's rating scale in the form of questions that someone might be asked during an evaluation interview. After using the rating scale, we go on to the fuller description of the symptoms and brief histories describing how these symptoms have appeared—or have been hidden—in patients we have treated. In elaborating on the description of depression we include symptoms that are not part of our initial self-rating questionnaire but that are commonly found among depressed persons. This extended description, with cases derived from actual patients, provides a clearer understanding of what we mean by vague terms such as "loss of pleasure" and "loss of energy." We also describe the symptoms of mania, a paradoxical form of depression commonly known as manic-depression (or bipolar disorder), and include a rating scale for mania as well. Later in the chapter we turn to mild forms of depression and of manic-depression.

We want to emphasize again that this is not a self-help book that will teach people to diagnose themselves. We want to help people learn the warning signals so that they can decide whether they should seek a diagnosis from a qualified professional. Individuals (sometimes aided by their families or others close to them) are in the best possible position to detect changes—possibly dangerous ones—in themselves. The rating scales and methods of scoring follow. (For rating someone close to you rather than yourself, think of how the scale might apply to that person.)

Self-Rating Scale for Depression

Have either of the following symptoms been present nearly every day for *at least two weeks?*

A.1. Have you been sad, blue, or "down in the dumps"?

A.2. Have you lost interest or pleasure in all or almost all the things you usually do (work, hobbies, other activities)?

If *either* A.1. or A.2. is true, continue. If not, you probably do not have a depressive illness.

Have any of the following been present nearly every day for *at least two weeks?*

1. A poor appetite or overeating?   No   Yes

2. Insomnia?   No   Yes

3. Oversleeping? (Going to bed earlier than
   usual, staying in bed later than usual,
   taking naps?)   No   Yes

4. Do you have low energy, fatigue, or
   chronic tiredness?   No   Yes

5. Are you less active or talkative than
   usual or do you feel slowed down or
   restless?   No   Yes

6. Do you avoid the company of other
   people?   No   Yes

7. Do you lose interest or enjoyment in
   sex and other pleasurable activities?   No   Yes

8. Do you fail to experience pleasure
   when you are praised, given presents,
   promoted, etc.?   No   Yes

9. Do you have feelings of inadequacy or
   decreased feelings of self-esteem, or are
   you increasingly self-critical?   No   Yes

10. Are you less efficient or do you accomplish
    less at school, work, or home?   No   Yes

11. Do you feel less able to cope with the
    routine responsibilities of everyday life?   No   Yes

12. Do you find that your concentration is
    poor or that you have difficulty making
    decisions (even trivial ones)?   No   Yes

If A.1 or A.2 is true, and if you answer Yes to any four of these
twelve questions, you *probably* have a depressive illness and

should consult a qualified physician. Even if you have only two or three symptoms, you should seriously consider a checkup. One reason we say that you probably have a depressive illness is that some people with these symptoms have a physical illness such as anemia or low thyroid activity. When you seek professional help for a possible depressive illness, it is important that your physician makes sure that you have a complete physical checkup at the same time.

The psychiatrist will also try to determine whether you may be going through a temporary upset due to life circumstances and do not really have a biological depression.

In deciding whether or not you have depressive illness, you should try not to give too much weight to what may seem to you to be plausible reasons for your bad feelings. Life is never perfect, and if people look hard enough, they can find some reason for feeling bad. Even a major loss, such as a death in the family or a divorce, may not be the real reason for your depressed emotional state. Furthermore, depressive illness itself may make people less capable of dealing with life's problems and may actually lead to life stresses, such as the loss of a job or the breakup of a relationship. In such instances what looks like the cause of depression may actually be one of its results. Depressive illness is often triggered by a real event—the death of a loved one, for example—but still requires treatment.

Depressive illnesses are easiest to recognize when someone has a sudden change in his or her emotional state for no apparent reason. People who find themselves saying, "I can't understand why I feel so bad. There is no good reason for it," always need a diagnostic review. However, depressive illnesses may develop gradually, so that the patient doesn't see any big difference between her current emotional state and how she felt a few years ago. Such a person may think her depressed mood is simply her normal state—"perhaps I am just a pessimistic and introverted person." Even prolonged chronic depressions, which have been thought of as the person's normal response to life, may nevertheless respond to medical treatment.

One rule of thumb involves the length of the period of distress and the degree of trouble that it has produced. If the distress has lasted for over a month, or if family, employment, or social life have been substantially affected, a checkup is highly advisable. However, even those who have been feeling apathetic for only a few weeks, or who can handle their usual activities only by great effort, should also consider a checkup.

There are several sorts of depressive illness, and there are many different degrees of severity. As we indicated, someone with depressive illness may not have all of the symptoms in the rating scale. Nonetheless, if some of these symptoms are all too familiar, you should not put off getting help.

Therefore, rate yourself on the symptoms with an open mind. If the rating scale indicates that you may have a depressive illness, you should get a checkup, regardless of any social or psychological explanations that occur to you.

To provide a more vivid picture of how symptoms of these kinds affect people's lives, we present a series of disguised excerpts from case histories of patients we have treated. Each of these patients has different symptoms of depression. In indicating how the symptoms manifested themselves in their lives, we return from time to time to some of the patients to continue their story because each kind of depression involves a different combination of symptoms and reveals itself in slightly different ways.

Recurrent Problems in Patients' Illnesses

Loss of Interest

The symptoms of sadness and loss of interest in life are two highly important aspects of depressive illness. Most people who are depressed will say they are sad or blue or down in the dumps. Many will say that they have lost interest in everything. A few people with a depressive illness are not sad or blue but instead have widespread loss of interest in their usual pursuits. These people may not recognize themselves as depressed, but this symptom is a critical one.

People have a wide variety of interests and pleasures in their lives—including, usually, simple biological pleasures such as eating and sex. People also look forward to family gatherings, sports, vacations, social activities, hobbies, and, in general, to the possibility that good things will be happening. When they think of future pleasant events, they usually have a sense of warm, optimistic hopefulness that is itself already a pleasant feeling.

Many depressed people lose these warm feelings and experience a sharp decrease in the ability to have pleasure. The technical term for this is *anhedonia*. Activities that used to excite become boring or unrewarding. Good food may taste like cardboard, and those suffering depression may just pick at their meals. In severe depression, patients lose the ability to feel and reciprocate love. They do not experience warmth toward the people who mean the most to them. In addition, there is a loss of sexual desire and responsivity. Formerly satisfactory sexual relationships become unstimulating and burdensome. The depressed individual feels apathetic and unreactive, and may have a diminished capacity to be close to others.

Mood is a pervasive sustained emotion that markedly affects our view of the world. Such moods include anger, anxiety, elation, and depression. Normal mood varies, depending on circumstances. Rewarding lives result in animated, outgoing moods. If things turn sour, then mood becomes subdued, cautious, and somewhat indifferent. When things go well again, the usual good feelings are restored.

Depressed people are different from people whose unhappiness is an obviously appropriate response to life circumstances. The mood of a depressed person is not in tune with the environment. Some severely depressed people are completely unresponsive to what is really good in their lives. It is not uncommon for depressed people to be told that they need a vacation or a change of pace only to find that, when they go on a trip, they continue to feel bad.

Other depressed people can be temporarily cheered up. They will often crave attention and social stimulation because that is the only way they can lift their spirits and alter their moods. However, what marks them as having an illness is the fact that, without continued excitement and praise, their mood slumps.

The cases given derive from actual case histories, with changes made in identifying details. At times, several cases have been combined for the sake of succinctness. In all cases, the symptoms described have been repeatedly demonstrated in the scientific clinical literature.

■ *Jill Jason*, a busy young housewife and mother, found herself increasingly indifferent about her usual activities at home and in the community. She stopped going to her bridge club, was bored by television, was unsympathetic to her husband's difficulties and triumphs, and just went through the motions with the children. She complained, "I don't know what's gotten into me. Everything was going so well. Now I don't give a damn, and I can't snap out of it. My son came home with all A's on his report card and I couldn't care less."

Jill's mood was particularly bad in the morning. Sometimes late at night she got a kick out of watching television. But by the next morning, everything seemed awful again. Her husband began to complain that she never enjoyed anything anymore, that even her sense of humor had disappeared.

When a doctor told Jill that she had been working too hard and needed a change of scene, she went to a resort with her husband. However, the vacation was a total disaster. Jill participated in a few activities and then stopped going altogether. She spent most of the time sitting in their room. She let her husband drag her to the swimming pool a few times because she had always loved to swim, but now she got nothing out of it.

■ *Mary Malloy* was a vivacious young receptionist who ordinarily loved dating and romance and had had a long string of boyfriends. After a series of unexpected disappointments, she found herself less interested in going out. She spent more and more time alone. She told her friends that life was a rat race and that she was growing up. However, she was also losing interest in her work.

Mary was at her best in the morning. She would get up, cook breakfast, and get to work by 8:30 AM. At that time she enjoyed applying herself and solving problems. However, by midafternoon she knew that she was just shuffling papers around. By the time she was ready to leave the office in the evening, she could accomplish nothing.

Mary spent a lot of time quietly in bed. However, when friends came over she would brighten and become animated. Frequently they tried to talk her into going to a party, to cheer her up. She usually refused, saying that parties were dull and there wasn't any point to them.

Surprisingly, when she did agree to go out, she seemed to have fun and was almost her old self. But when she got home she slumped into her low mood again. After one of these experiences, when her friends tried to persuade her to go to another party, she said that she wouldn't go because parties were boring. Her friends reminded her that she had seemed to enjoy the last party, but Mary insisted that she really didn't feel up to it.

Finally, like Jill Jason, Mary was persuaded to go to a resort for a change. At first it seemed like the right prescription. She danced, played tennis, met some new attractive men, and exchanged phone numbers. Her old zest for life seemed to return. However, when she went back to the city her level of interest slowly declined. She didn't call her new friends, and when they called her, she saw them a few times but then let the relationships fizzle out.

■ *Milton Meyer* was a successful surgeon in his forties who also enjoyed teaching. He was an avid amateur violinist as well as an enthusiastic gardener. Long before he noticed anything unusual, his wife observed gradual changes. His interest in surgery lessened and he disparaged his work, saying that it was not very useful in the long run, that it only patched things up. He found reasons for avoiding teaching, stopped playing in his amateur quartet, and hired someone to take care of his garden. His wife sensed his increasing withdrawal, but when she asked him whether he was depressed, he denied it. In terms of how he felt, he was being honest. He was not sad, blue, or down in the dumps—he had just lost interest in everything.

■ *Sally* and *Jane Harris* were cousins who had led charmed lives. Their fathers were brothers who had maintained close personal and business ties, their families were warm, stimulating, and protective. Their economic circumstances were excellent, and both families could afford to send the young women to the best schools, where their fine minds showed themselves to good advantage. Sally decided to become a doctor and Jane to become a lawyer. They both worked hard, achieved recognition, and made very favorable careers. They had deferred marriage to continue their advanced education, but both had long-term intimate relationships and both eventually did marry, once life's circumstances had solidified and they had achieved their career goals.

When the cousins were in their early thirties, their fathers, traveling together on a business trip, died in the crash of a small commuter plane, leaving the entire extended family crushed and bereft. Both Sally and Jane cried for days; they sat around brooding, preoccupied with their loss, thinking excessively and painfully of their fathers. Their mothers too were racked with acute grief. Whenever the family got together, they would immediately start to cry without saying a single word.

Despite their torment, both women rose to the occasion and continued to go to work, to carry out their professional duties, to take care of their patients and clients, to supervise their households, to love and care for their husbands and children. All this was uphill work, but they did it. Moreover, with time, both found that immersing themselves in everyday details was a consolation, as it distracted them from their constant gnawing grief. Both learned that the best medicine for their grief was turning their minds outward toward activities.

After some three months, Sally's emotional life had pretty much resumed its former richness, though punctuated by occasional waves of longing for her dead father. Jane on the other hand, when she talked to Sally, told her that she never thought about her father any more. As a matter of act, her formerly active imagination about both the good and bad things in her life seemed somewhat dulled. Previously, she had spent a great deal of time reading law journals to be sure that she was absolutely on top of current decisions, but lately she had let this slide.

Loss of Energy

Most of the time people have a feeling of zest, of get-up-and-go. When things interest them, they feel energized and will pursue their goals actively. Depressed people feel as if they have run out of gas. They complain about fatigue, feel that everything is an effort, that they just can't get going, that their body feels heavy or leaden, that they are listless and slowed down. They find themselves unable to achieve their usual goals.

■ *Jill Jason* started to complain that she was weary all the time. She was usually efficient and well organized, but now she procrastinated with her work, putting off tasks that had to be done around the house. Because of her lack of interest and lack of energy, she became progressively withdrawn socially. When her friends told her that she needed vitamins or a tonic, she tried them, but they didn't help.

■ *Mary Malloy* expected to hear from her remaining boyfriend one Friday about weekend plans, but he didn't call. Suddenly she was overcome by overwhelming fatigue. Her body felt made of lead. Previously she had been uninterested in making a special effort to engage in various activities, but now she felt physically incapable of moving. She crawled into bed, where she spent the entire weekend eating Oreos.

■ *Sally Harris* had resumed her meaningful 60-hour work week, dividing her time between her private office, the clinic that she worked in, and the hospital. Although she complained about work, it was in a good-humored spirit and, in fact, her heavy schedule was almost entirely self-imposed, not because of financial need but rather because of a deep interest in her work and patients.

■ *Jane Harris* also was used to working overtime. In fact, her legal firm billed their clients by actually monitoring time spent working on each case. They had an intricate system of clocking on and off time spent reading, conferring, writing, on the phone, in court, etc.

Jane was somewhat surprised, although it did not come as a complete shock, when her boss pointed out to her that her billings were falling off. Peculiarly, during the period of her intense grief, her billings, if anything, had gone up as she had plunged into her work to ease her pain. Now, although still productive, she just was not putting in as much time as before. She told her boss that maybe she was suffering from a mild case of burnout; legal technicalities that formerly intrigued and challenged her now seemed somewhat dull and routine. Furthermore, she just didn't seem to have the zest for it anymore. When she looked at the work piled up in her in-box, she began to feel oppressed rather than assertive about her capacities to deal with difficult work.

Appetite and Weight Disturbances:
Changes in Eating Patterns

For most people, food is one of the greatest pleasures. It is common knowledge that appetite disturbances accompany all sorts of illnesses. This seems particularly true of depression. Some people eat more when depressed, and some eat less.

■ *Mary Malloy* spent a great deal of time at home alone as she became more withdrawn. She watched television and ate junk food. She had a particularly strong craving for sweets, carbohydrates, and chocolate. She gained fifteen pounds, which added to her feelings of self-disgust and her unwillingness to try to be socially active. At times she would stuff herself with so much candy that she would force herself to throw up to relieve her bloating. Mary had read some pop psychology that told her that she was acting infantile because eating was the only way she could feel loved.

■ *Jill Jason*, in contrast, just pecked at her food. She said that nothing tasted good and ignored even her favorite dishes. Her husband told her that she would get really sick if she didn't eat, so she would make a real effort to get something down every day. To her, eating was a chore, and at times she just couldn't do it. She was getting very thin.

Sleep Disturbances

People differ in their need for sleep and in their sleep patterns. Temporary difficulties in falling asleep, particularly when under tension, are common. Some people experience various patterns of broken sleep, commonly referred to as *insomnia*. But many depressives fall asleep with ease only to have restless sleep and early morning awakening. Others seem to require remarkably large amounts of sleep. Although it is clear that not everyone with sleep irregularities is depressed, changes in sleep patterns frequently accompany depressions and are a vital warning sign.

■ *Jill Jason*, although fearful and upset, had little difficulty falling asleep. As a matter of fact, she welcomed sleep since it gave her some relief. Nevertheless, she would awaken several times in the middle of the night and feel awful. Her gloom and feelings of hopelessness were at their worst. After much tossing and turning, she would eventually fall back to sleep. Finally, at five in the morning she would awaken and find it impossible to go back to sleep even though she felt exhausted.

■ *Mary Malloy*, as she became less and less interested in her life, was sleeping more and more. When working, she had waves of fatigue and sleepiness that prevented her from doing her job properly. Finally, she quit work and stayed at home, where she took frequent naps or simply dozed in bed all day. She explained her behavior by saying she was retreating from reality.

Other Physical Symptoms

Periods of pain and bodily distress are usually signs of illness. Most such difficulties are temporary, and people usually shrug them off or take it easy for a while until they go away. If sufficiently distressed they may seek medical attention.

The tendency to seek medical attention is quite variable. Some people consider it a sign of weakness to seek help or to complain, so they minimize their difficulties and discomfort (they "tough it out" in a stoical way). Others find their distress too difficult to bear alone and frequently turn to friends, family, clergy, or doctors for help.

Most people can't stand the idea that they may have a disturbance of their emotions or feelings, since they think that would label them as crazy. Therefore, when they are in distress, they find it far easier to believe that something is physically wrong with them than to recognize that they are having emotional problems.

■ *Jill Jason's* husband was losing patience. He finally told her that if she didn't go to her family doctor her would drag her there. Jill then told him that she thought she might have cancer. She had all these weak feelings and was losing weight. Every once in a while she felt funny all over, as if she might faint. She had been brooding about the possibility of cancer for several months but was afraid to mention it because that might make it come true. She was afraid to find out what the doctor might discover.

When she finally went for a physical examination, her doctor found no signs of cancer or any other physical illness. Although she was obviously haggard, underweight, and miserable, he told her that there was nothing wrong with her and that she should buck up, pull herself together, and stop feeling so sorry for herself. On the way home, Jill said that she still thought she had cancer and that the doctor had missed it.

■ *Mary Malloy* thought that she had heart disease. Every once in a while her heart would go a mile a minute, and she would feel as if her head was floating off her shoulders and that she might fall down any second. Several times she had such difficulty in catching her breath that she thought she was dying and went to an emergency room. They told her that her heart was fine and it was just her nerves.

One doctor suggested that she take tranquilizers for her attacks of panic, and, after much hesitation, she took some. They seemed to help slightly, but she was still weary, fatigued, and socially isolated; occasionally she again thought she was having a heart attack. Her family thought she was playing for sympathy.

■ *Bob Bush*, a successful producer of Broadway shows, for no apparent reason, developed a low-grade, chronic bellyache. Sometimes he would feel as if he had diarrhea and would suddenly have to rush to the bathroom. He found himself so preoccupied with this that he was not doing justice to the theatrical enterprises he was producing. Wherever he went, the first thing he would do was check out where the bathroom was. He began to avoid long trips. His social life became progressively more constricted as he made excuses not to go to places where he would not have ready access to a bathroom.

Bob went to many different doctors, who all told him that there was nothing wrong with his physical health and that he was being silly. He began to feel sad and withdrawn but blamed this on his physical troubles.

■ *Saul Schwartz*, a middle-aged businessman who usually enjoyed life, said there was nothing wrong with him even though he hadn't worked for the past two months. He didn't see what all the fuss was about because it was his terrible backache that kept him from working. The doctor had told him that he couldn't find anything wrong with his back and that he was sure the pain would go away in time. Saul was simply waiting for the pain to go away. His married son, David, kept telling him that something must be wrong besides his back because he wasn't even reading the newspapers anymore and he had gotten very quiet.

David was worried because when he persuaded his father to come out for a ride or to go to the movies, Saul didn't enjoy himself. Who would enjoy themselves if they had a bad back? Saul had never been a complainer and he wasn't complaining now. He didn't even talk about his back. He only mentioned it when people told him he should be trying to do more. Saul's wife asked him whether he was depressed, because he seemed so blue and quiet. Saul said that he wasn't sad or blue but was just quiet because of his back.

Decreased Sexual Drive

■ *Jill Jason* and her husband had been passionate and sexually involved in the first few years of their marriage. With time, the frequency and fervor had diminished some, but the gamut of sexual activity from casual caresses through lovemaking was still central to their lives. Both looked forward to vacations knowing that the break in routine would be heightened by a burst of renewed ardor.

As Jill steadily lost interest in her usual activities, she showed less enthusiasm for sexual intercourse. Her husband sensed that she seemed to feel that their previously enjoyable sexual relationship had now become an unpleasant chore. An attempt to renew the honeymoon spirit by taking a long weekend trip was a miserable fiasco. Jill said she wasn't just dead sexually, she was dead everywhere.

Restlessness or Slowing Down: Changes in Movement and Speech Patterns

Everyone has an individual pattern of speech and motion. Some people are quiet, whereas others talk a lot. Some people are active and restless, while others can sit contentedly for long periods. Depressive illness often markedly changes these patterns.

■ *Jill Jason* was getting quieter and quieter and more and more immobile. Her family would find her sitting for hours in a chair, looking blankly at the wall. When they asked her how she was feeling, she seemed at first not to hear them, but after a marked delay she spoke a few words in a weak voice. She said nothing spontaneously. Her family thought she just wanted to be left alone, so they left her alone.

■ *Peggy Pearl*, a wealthy, middle-aged housewife with an active social life, couldn't stop talking or pacing. As her husband came through the door, she assailed him with complaints about herself, about him, about the neighbors and the family. She felt so bad that he had to do something immediately because she just couldn't go on like this. She nervously paced around the apartment wringing her hands and picking at her cuticles. At times she got so upset that she pulled her hair out.

Self-Reproach and Guilt: Loss of Self-Esteem and Painful Mood and Thought Content

Low self-esteem is usually not recognized as one of the most common symptoms of depression. On the whole, most people think well of themselves. Most people know that they are not extraordinarily charming, not strikingly handsome or beautiful, not brilliant or talented, but they are satisfied with themselves anyway. They can usually think of something they're good at and somebody who wants to be with them. Despite current popular ideas to the contrary—fostered by television talk shows, movies, books, and magazines—most people are optimistic and adaptable, even under difficult circumstances.

If someone has failed to reach his goals, or has been rejected or put down by loved ones, that may result in temporary bad feelings about himself. But such feelings rarely last long, and they usually force the person into some form of constructive activity.

Since depressed people view the future pessimistically and are unable to respond positively, even to good news and stimulating activities, it is not surprising that many conclude that it is all their fault and they are ineffectual losers. Such feelings are often explained psychologically on the grounds that such people must have been treated badly by their parents, who left them with permanent psychological scars.

The wretched mood that characterizes depressives is often accompanied by negative emotions and thoughts about themselves. They may brood about their failures and feel worthless and self-critical. These feelings may become so painful that the depressed person simply cannot stand herself and is plagued by thoughts of guilt over past failures. She begins to feel that she is being punished and should expect punishment, and that perhaps she would be better off dead.

The intense painfulness of many depressions is difficult for the ordinary person to appreciate. Therefore, when a depressed person tries to communicate about how bad she feels, she is often criticized because it looks like some sort of act or put-on.

■ *Jill Jason* told her husband that she thought she was a terrible person and a failure as a mother and wife, and then she cried bitterly. Initially sympathetic, her husband told her that he loved her, that the whole family loved her, and that everyone thought she was a wonderful person. At first this seemed to help her, but the next day she felt as bad as ever and complained constantly again.

After a while Jill's husband became thoroughly irritated. No matter what he said or did, it didn't work, leaving him feeling helpless and overwhelmed. At times he got quite angry at her. "Why are you behaving this way? You've had everything anyone should want." He couldn't help feeling that his wife was like a bottomless pit that nothing could fill.

■ *Jane* and *Sally Harris* frequently met to talk over their families and friends and inevitably their common loss. Slowly the tenor of their conversation shifted. Sally reminisced about her father and the good times they had, how helpful he was to her, the pride he had taken in her and his understanding ways. She was filled with thoughts of her loss. Jane, on the other hand, talked less and less about her father and more and more about how bad she felt, how uninteresting her work had become, and how she was feeling more and more guilty about letting her family and her boss down. When she did talk about her father, she would often dwell upon how she should have been a better daughter. Sally would point out to her that her relationship with her father had been just great, but Jane didn't see it that way.

Poor Concentration and Indecisiveness: Mental Difficulties

Many people have small fluctuations in their ability to concentrate. When fatigued, they find it more difficult to concentrate and to stay focused. Depressed people have many complaints about their mental functioning. They feel that their memory is shot and that they cannot pay attention. In addition, they often behave in an extremely indecisive and perplexed fashion, as if they just can't figure things out.

Most nonimpulsive people deliberate carefully about major decisions, such as whether to accept or quit a job, or whether or not to get married. Indecisiveness is a symptom of depression when individuals cannot make up their minds about relatively trivial matters. An example would be a woman who is about to go out to dinner with friends but who delays the group's departure for half an hour because she cannot decide whether she wants to eat at a French or Italian restaurant.

■ *Jill Jason* had been the mainstay of her church group. When a social event or dinner had to be arranged, she was a take-charge, get-it-done person. Now when she was asked to organize a church supper, she felt completely overwhelmed. She couldn't decide whether she should do it or not and kept wavering back and forth. When her husband told her with exasperation that she had managed such events ten times before without trouble, she stared at him blankly and started to cry helplessly. Jill's husband told the church group that she couldn't do it, hoping that she would feel less burdened, but that didn't help, either. She persisted in feeling overwhelmed, incompetent, and indecisive.

Deterioration of Social Relationships

Most people have a network of friends and family members whom they depend on for help when trouble strikes. Typically, they rely on little informal mutual-aid societies and get much of their joy in life from their friends and lovers. Depression sabotages these relationships, so that family and longtime friends begin to drift away.

■ *Jill Jason* had stopped going to bridge parties. At first her friends came to visit, but she was silent and unresponsive. When they would joke with her, trying to cheer her up, she didn't crack a smile, When they told her that she'd be all right soon, she just shook her head. She didn't return their calls and visits, and after a while they rarely called. Her husband started to stay out late after work because her dissatisfaction with everything made him feel helpless and frustrated.

■ *Mary Malloy* still enjoyed her relationship with her boyfriend. Because that was the only real source of pleasure that she still had, she became very greedy and demanding about it. When her boyfriend told her that he would call her at 9:00 PM but called at 9:15 because his train had been delayed, she burst into tears and told him that he couldn't treat her so cruelly. He should know how bad she felt and how much she looked forward to seeing him and how her whole life depended on him and his love for her, and where would she be without him? Under such pressure he eventually stopped seeing her.

■ *Peggy Pearl* got nasty. She told her husband that it was all his fault that she felt so terrible and that everyone had let her down. She complained incessantly that nobody loved her or wanted her or paid any attention to her. After a while she was right.

■ *Jane Harris* had managed to be a superwoman by many people's standards. She had a successful career, a happy home life, and wide circle of friends and activities. People would wonder at her remarkable ability, vivacity, and charm. Lately, however, things had been narrowing in. She wasn't working as hard, entertaining as much, or livening her family with good-natured banter. She was quieter and the social circle was steadily constricting. She called on fewer and fewer of her friends, accepted fewer and fewer social engagements. Several of her friends said that it was no surprise to them, after all she had set herself an impossible task in life. Her growing depression was not perceived as an impairment of her truly extraordinary ability, but simply as what could be expected from anyone.

■ *Sally Harris*, in contrast, was still functioning at the same high level. She had an argument once with one of Jane's friends when Sally mentioned that Jane seemed to be doing poorly. Jane's friend said that it was not doing poorly to be working and running a household. Sally pointed out that you couldn't compare Jane with the average person because she wasn't average to start out with. Jane's impairment was only made obvious when you compared her current functioning with her former vibrant outgoing self. Jane's friend was unconvinced, Jane's life still looked pretty good to her. Sally, however, was getting more and more worried about her cousin.

For both Mary and Peggy, depression led to increased demands that could not be satisfied, and it drove others away. Jill's unresponsiveness had the same effect. But Jane's depression went undetected, except to her cousin Sally.

Increased Use of Intoxicants and Drugs

Alcohol and more recently marijuana are commonly consumed for recreational purposes. Most people can use these substances in moderation without too much difficulty. However, many people are unable to control their consumption of liquor and drugs, developing patterns of overuse that may destroy their lives.

Why some people can remain social drinkers while others become alcoholics is not fully understood. At least part of the answer is that some are suffering from depression and are using alcohol or marijuana as mental anesthetics and temporary distractions. They are really attempting to medicate themselves. However, because these substances do not lift the depression, they increase their consumption of them in their search for relief.

■ *Peggy Pearl*'s husband was astonished one night when he came home to find Peggy drunk. He and Peggy often had a couple of drinks, but the only time he had ever seen her drunk was after a big New Year's Eve party. He certainly didn't think that she ever drank during the day.

When Peggy sobered up she told him that she had just felt so bad that day, so lonely and isolated, that she thought maybe a little drink would help her out, and indeed it did. However, she hadn't expected to polish off the whole bottle. She said she wouldn't do it again, but she did, and increasingly often.

■ *Ralph Rogers*, an outstanding high-school student, was the pride of his family. He was captain of the high-school football team and near the top of his class. Everyone knew that Ralph had a big future ahead of him. Then Ralph's marks began to slip. He said that it was hard for him to concentrate, but actually he was spending less time at his studies. His teammates started to complain about him because his judgment on the field seemed impaired. He called the wrong plays and didn't respond rapidly when the other team tried something new.

Ralph began to hang out with a different crowd who used drugs. In time, he began to use marijuana steadily and started to cut classes. The school principal finally called his parents in and told them sadly that Ralph seemed to have a drug problem.

Vocational Failure

In the same way that Ralph Rogers dramatically manifested a loss of competence in his school activities, prosperous business executives and hardworking professionals may also suddenly become ineffective.

■ *Richard Rogers*, Ralph's father, a prosperous sales manager, was upset about his son's difficulties. He felt that somehow he had let Ralph down and was to blame. At work he became lost in guilty ruminations. Previously decisive and energetic, he now had trouble making up his mind about everything. His co-workers, who depended on him, became very dissatisfied, and finally his boss told him that he'd better snap out of it.

Richard tried without success to return to his previous level of functioning. He knew that brooding about Ralph's difficulties did his son no good, and wasn't helping him either, but he just couldn't stop it. He was starting to wake up at night, and his appetite was vanishing.

Hostility and Irritability

Some people think that an inability to express anger causes depression. They even argue that depression is anger turned back against oneself. This particular theory ignores the fact that, in the midst of depressive periods, many people are far more irritable and angry than usual. Moreover, their irritability may get worse when such people suspect that they may be suffering some emotional problem but are not yet read to admit it.

■ *Richard Rogers* had always been easy to work for. He rarely snapped at anyone, and even when he had to chastise one of his salesmen for goofing off, he always did it in a straightforward way. He didn't angrily bawl out the salesman but simply tried to change his bad habits and improve his productivity.

Lately, however, he was barking at everyone. Even the slightest error, of no real consequence, provoked a tirade. His secretary of 20 years finally told him that he was causing a lot of trouble. She was shocked when he told her to shut up and mind her own business.

■ *Peggy Pearl* was becoming impossible to live with. Everything caused an argument. She was upset when her children didn't visit and berated them over the phone. When they did visit, she yelled at them for not visiting more often.

Peggy fired her longtime maid, accusing her of getting uppity. She fired the next maid because she couldn't learn fast enough where things were. She fired still another maid because she didn't like her expression. She spent a lot of time talking about how you can't get decent help anymore. When she and her husband went to restaurants she often got into embarrassing fights with the waiters, saying the food was never any good. Her continued excessive drinking made her temper even worse.

Peggy's husband, Bob, told her that he thought that something was definitely wrong with her. She used to be so sweet and helpful, but now she complained about others all the time. Peggy said that she had every reason to complain because she had discovered how lousy everyone was, including her husband. Look at the way her so-called friends had stopped calling her.

When Bob dragged Peggy to the family doctor, the doctor said that there wasn't anything obviously wrong with her, but since she had felt so bad for a year now, maybe she ought to see a colleague of his for a consultation. When Peggy asked what the colleague's specialty was, the doctor answered that she was a nerve doctor.

"You think I'm crazy," yelled Peggy. "No." said the doctor, "I just think you might need a little help in getting yourself together." "You want to put me away," Peggy whimpered. "I'm crazy." "Look Peggy," said the doctor, "we just want you to talk with somebody for a while. It will help you feel better."

Peggy said that she would think about it, but she didn't go.

Distortion of Reality

Our moods color our understanding of the world and ourselves. When we feel down, the world seems less satisfactory, and we seem less admirable. When we are up, the world is an interesting place, and we think we're pretty good. Depression causes major distortions in our perception of reality, and therefore makes handling our problems even more difficult.

■ *Richard Rogers* went into a real funk when his boss told him that he better snap out of it. He finally told the boss that he was quitting because he couldn't stand letting everyone down. The boss was astonished. He told Richard that he only meant that Richard should get some help. He added that Richard had been one of his best workers for many years, and he certainly had no intention of firing him. Richard repeated that he just wasn't up to it, thinking that he would surely be fired soon, he stopped going to work.

Dealing with the Future: Hopelessness, Suicidal Thoughts, and Suicide Attempts

When normal people think about the future, their feelings are a mixture of pluses and minuses. When they think about past happy events or imagine pleasant future possibilities, they have positive, warm feelings of recollection or anticipation. Many of us spend a lot of time daydreaming, which is nothing more than making ourselves feel good by thinking that the future might work out in ways that we would like. Such daydreams are often constructive since thinking about possibilities that produce good feelings may stir one into related realistic activity. This is what we mean by saying that a person is in a hopeful frame of mind and acting in an enterprising way.

When people think about past unhappy events and possible future difficulties, their mood is taken over by tension and apprehension. However, sometimes when they perceive trouble coming and feel anxious about it, they are also stirred into useful action. They think about possible maneuvers that will prevent the trouble from occurring or will at least remove them from the scene of probable pain. Once people have figured out a good strategy for avoiding impending trouble, their sense of hopefulness returns and they attempt to carry out their protective plans.

The depressed person has a marked decrease in the ability to remember and imagine pleasant thoughts. When he thinks about the future or the past, all he focuses on are the minuses. The pluses don't get through or are greatly reduced. Therefore, depressed persons cannot feel pleasant hopefulness.

A severe inability to feel optimism may lead to suicide. Since our attempts to deal with the future are steered by our hopeful thinking, the depressed person's loss of hope prevents him from planning constructively. He feels overwhelmed and helpless. When this feeling becomes too painful, many depressed people feel they would be better off dead. They would no longer be a burden to their family and they would no longer have to suffer such pain. Sometimes when they express such feelings, family and friends tend not to take them seriously. It is commonly thought that people who talk about suicide don't actually take their own lives, but this is simply not true.

■ *Gil Green* thought that he was a total failure. Although he had been an expert technician for many years, he became convinced that the new technology was just getting too difficult. He couldn't work and stayed home, brooding and spending much of his time in solitary drinking. One day he told his wife that he would be better off dead, but when she became upset, he hastened to reassure her that he didn't mean it. However, a week later he repeated the threat while intoxicated. Frightened, his wife insisted that he see a doctor.

Gil told the doctor that it was just the liquor talking, that he was just kidding and that being out of work would upset anybody. The doctor did not spend the time to review Gil's feelings in depth. In particular, he did not inquire as to Gil's sense of hopelessness, inability to enjoy himself, sleep disturbance, and increasing use of alcohol. He hurriedly suggested that Gil take a tranquilizer. A few days later, Gil's wife came home from a trip to the grocery store and found him hanging from a basement beam. His suicide note said that it wasn't her fault but that the future was hopeless and that he couldn't stand letting everybody down.

Depressive Reactions to Threatening Life Events

The patients described here, despite their differences, all have in common depressive symptoms that do not seem related to disastrous life events. In the two examples that follow, the depressions followed unfortunate life circumstances. Nevertheless, these depressions differ *qualitatively* from each other, as we will explore when we look at the treatment of these patients.

George Gelb, and others who are discussed here, came to a university depression clinic to participate in a study that was evaluating a new experimental antidepressant. The way such studies are done is that the patient may receive, without knowing which, either the new experimental antidepressant, or a standard antidepressant, or a dummy pill, which is called a *placebo*. Doctors who evaluate the effects of the treatment also do not know which pill the patient is receiving. The reason for this is that some people will get better because their depression is improving on its own or because they respond to the simple fact of receiving help. Including the placebo pill allows the doctors to find out how many of their patients would have gotten better without specific treatment. Comparing the effects of the standard antidepressant tells one how much benefit that drug produced over and above the effects of just receiving a placebo and coming for help. The experimental antidepressant can then be compared both with the standard antidepressant and the placebo to see if it is effective and whether it is better than usual treatment.

■ *George Gelb* was a 51-year-old high-middle management executive in a large corporation. He came to a depression clinic to participate in a study comparing the effects of a placebo, a standard antidepressant, and an experimental antidepressant. For several years his marriage had been deteriorating, and a few months earlier his foreign-born wife had informed him that she planned to return to her native country, taking their 14-year-old daughter and as much of their money as she could get. Shortly thereafter, his corporation had decided to reduce output by 75 percent. George would be laid off, receiving only a few months' pay. His management job was so specialized that he doubted whether he could find another like it.

At the first interview, the psychiatrist saw a middle-aged man whose lined face and slow-moving, bent-over posture reflected his inner state. In a voice filled with tears he described his marital and vocational disasters. The symptoms were typical: guilt, pervasive loss of interest, great fatigue, seriously disrupted sleep, appetite and weight loss. Severely depressed, George was entered in the drug study.

■ *Carl Carr*, a 31-year-old computer repairman, contacted a psychiatrist approximately a year and a half after the development of a depression. His computer-repair work involved being in South America for periods of three to four months followed by periods of about the same length in the United States. The depression had developed after he had sustained a hand injury that interfered with his ability to perform his job. Despite excellent medical care, the injury was recovering so slowly that he could not work.

Prior to his injury Carl had been a hardworking and competent young man who had many friends and married early. His major psychological difficulty had stemmed from his divorce. During his work-related travels his wife had gone through law school and had begun to feel that their lives were now too different. The marriage had been unexciting but had seemed stable, and Carl was surprised when his wife asked for a divorce. They tried marriage counseling, but it did not save the marriage. A few years later Carl fell in love with another woman, whom he planned to marry.

Following the injury Carl had vivid flashbacks of the accident and noted that he was becoming increasingly anxious and depressed. He returned to school in order to retool by obtaining another degree. For the first time he found school difficult and his concentration and memory impaired. He also began to have episodes of dizziness, light-headedness, and palpitations.

In seeking help, Carl first consulted a group of nonmedical psychotherapists, who recommended hypnotherapy along with "reality therapy" and "rational emotive therapy." He was perceived as depressed, but they recommended that antidepressants not be given because of the possible negative effect on his concentration. During the next year and a half he received intermittent psychotherapy while his condition worsened. His grades at school fell, he became anxious when he left the house (*agoraphobia*), and his self-esteem diminished "to the vanishing point." His psychological problems were worsened by his physical ones. His injured hand could not be repaired sufficiently to allow him to return to his job. At this point he consulted a psychiatrist.

Grief

In mentioning depressive responses to life events, it is important to discuss grief. Grief and mourning are normal psychological responses to the death of a loved one. Psychiatrists see the mourning process—thinking of, talking of, recalling experiences with the deceased—as a necessary part of healing. The pain and the attempt to deal with it enable the bereaved to begin to separate himself or herself from the deceased, to re-enter life, and to develop the ability to form new relationships.

In normal grief or bereavement, a person manifests symptoms very similar to those of biological depression, but there are some differences. Studies of the bereaved have shown that their most common symptoms are depressed mood, crying spells, insomnia, and weight loss. These symptoms are indistinguishable from those of depressive illness. One major and obvious difference, of course, is that the bereaved perceive their feelings as normal and comprehensible, and, for most, their functioning is unimpaired. The bereaved do not feel guilty, or if they do, their guilt is chiefly about things they wish they had done or not done preceding the death of the loved one. In general, the bereaved do not markedly slow down physically and mentally, and they do not experience decreases in self-esteem or increases in self-criticism. They may entertain thoughts that they would be better off dead or that they should have died with the deceased, but they are not preoccupied with thoughts of suicide. In some instances prolonged grief may merge into biological depression.

There is disagreement among psychologists and psychiatrists about how long "normal" bereavement should last. In general, if severe grief leads to progressive inability to function, grief may have developed into clinical depression. Some psychiatrists believe that antidepressant medication relieves the symptoms of "pathological grief," although antidepressant medication is ineffectual during the normal grieving process.

■   *Jane* and *Sally Harris* went out for lunch one day, and Sally observed that Jane was just picking at her food. Jane had gotten quite thin recently, and Sally finally decided to tell Jane of her concerns. She pointed out that Jane had slowed down, was hardly talking, had lost her sense of humor, and was becoming more and more isolated from her friends. Sally didn't know that Jane's work was not up to her former standards either. Sally asked Jane whether she was still grieving for her father and told Jane that she still cried at least once a week, thinking of her dad. Jane shocked her when she said that not only didn't she think about her father but that she couldn't cry. At times, she wished that she could cry, but rather than feeling pain, she felt empty. At that point, Sally's medical training took over and she suddenly realized that her cousin was not simply grief-stricken but had become ill with a major depression. That her illness had been triggered by a real-life loss was certainly true, and that Jane had never shown any sign of a previous predisposition to depression was also true. Nonetheless, Jane had passed beyond grief and now required medical care.

Jane told Sally that, as the product of an excellent upper-middle-class education, she had learned that emotional illness came from unconscious conflicts over repressed sexual and aggressive urges. In her readings, Jane even discovered that psychoanalysis taught that severe depression after the loss of a loved one was due to unconscious hatred for the loved one, which was now turned back against oneself. Further, she had read about antidepressants but thought that they were something like alcohol or tranquilizers, drugs that would just simply dull your senses and obliterate painful memories. Taking a pill was clearly second-class care that meant that you were just sweeping your troubles under the rug.

Jane told this to Sally and was surprised when her dear friend and cousin told her that she was nearly 40 years behind the times. Jane was especially surprised because she had considered herself a well-informed person who kept up-to-date by reading the best newspapers and magazines. They were full of articles describing psychological causes for emotional disturbance wholly dismissing biological approaches as crude and naïve. Sally told Jane about a colleague who specialized in depression and medication and insisted that she be evaluated immediately.

Long-Term Depression

The following case differs from the others in the long-term nature of the illness, which had been misdiagnosed in the patient's earlier years.

■   *Edith Ebel*, a 50-year-old married professional, was a participant in a drug study with a new antidepressant medication. She had been depressed for approximately ten years and had received two rounds of psychotherapy during that time. As a child and adolescent, she had had symptoms that were a first considered neurotic, the result of growing up in a difficult family.

Edith had been the oldest of four girls raised by a mother described as spoiled, demanding, and greedy, who became an alcoholic during the patient's early childhood and adolescence. The mother apparently did not feel and certainly did not express warm or loving feelings. She punished the patient with sarcasm and contempt. No help was available from Edith's father, who was a psychological absentee—he showed no interest in her.

The family lived in the country, and Edith had few friends— although those she had were close and she valued them highly. She dealt with the family situation by withdrawing and by mostly reading. A tall woman, she had gone through a particularly gawky adolescence, accurately described herself as unattractive, and did not begin to date until she entered college. Nevertheless, she made a fine marriage to a thoughtful, caring, and loving man.

Edith functioned well on a number of jobs and ran a ship-shape home. Her other major interest continued to be reading, and she also played some golf. She felt that she had been programmed to achieve and on her job was very competitive and sarcastic (she was aware of the irony of being like her mother), feeling adequate only when she could put down her peers. Unhappy at this situation, she finally entered psychotherapy.

At some time during her first psychotherapy, the quality of her mood changed. She lost interest in golf, her sex drive diminished, her irritability increased, and she began to behave unpleasantly to members of her family as well as to co-workers.

The two courses of psychotherapy, which together consumed more than three years spread out over almost a decade, convinced her that her problems were the result of her experiences, but she remained irritable and competitive, and still had few interests in life.

Mania

It is relatively easy to understand that depressed people are sick. They look miserable and often function poorly. Yet, strangely, many depressed patients at times feel excessively good. These periods are called "manic episodes," and sometimes manias occur when the patient has never been depressed. A person is considered manic if she (1) has a prolonged period during which she is euphoric, elevated, "flying"; and (2) has a number of the following symptoms: inflated self-esteem, or the feeling that she is better, wiser, superior to others; a markedly decreased need to sleep (for example, managing on a few hours a night); a tendency to monopolize conversations, talking rapidly and excessively; the feeling that her thoughts are flowing so rapidly that she cannot express them in an orderly fashion; increased activity—socially, at work or school, or sexually; impulsive behavior that often leads to trouble, such as buying sprees, promiscuity, and rash business decisions. Manic periods can be variable in duration, and frequently they are followed by severe depression, so that this combination of symptoms is commonly known as manic-depression.

Unlike the situation in depression, the manic patient, particularly if his mania is mild, may not recognize that he is ill. He perceives himself as enjoying life more than he ever has before, but those who know him often suspect that something is wrong. Before discussing mania, we will present the mania self-rating scale.

Self-Rating Scale for Mania

A1. Are you experiencing a distinct period of abnormally elevated and euphoric mood or unusually irritable and angry mood?

A2. During the period of mood disturbance, have you had any of the following symptoms?

1. Are you experiencing increased self-esteem or possible overevaluation of your abilities, achievement, or position in the world? Yes No

2. Do you have a decreased need for sleep? For example, if you ordinarily need 7 or 8 hours to function well, do you find that now you can feel perfectly alert and energetic on 3 or 4 hours sleep? Yes No

3. Are you increasingly talkative and do you feel an inner pressure to keep talking (or an inability to stop talking when it would be appropriate to do so)? Yes No

4. Do you find yourself rapidly shifting your conversation from one topic to another beginning on "X," taking off from that to "Y," taking off from that to "Z," etc. (with the inward feeling that your thoughts are racing)? Yes No

5. Are you increasingly distractible—is it difficult to focus or concentrate when necessary to do so, or are you easily drawn away to unimportant or irrelevant things (as trivial as the sounds of ice dropping in the icemaker or leaves blowing on the roof)?   Yes   No

6. Are you experiencing an increased sexual drive?   Yes   No

7. Are you overdoing things socially, voca-tionally, academically, or around the household—often to a clearly abnormal degree, for example, studying for much longer periods of time than necessary?   Yes   No

8. Are you overactive and restless? Are you unable to sit still comfortably so that you need to be constantly up and about?   Yes   No

9. Are you acting impulsively and over-optimistically in seeking pleasure and taking large risks? This is, are you pursuing what you like without weighing the risks to yourself—for example, going on unrestrained buying sprees, initiating indiscreet sexual relationships, or embarking on what may be foolish business invest-ments?*   Yes   No

If your answer to A is Yes, and if you answer Yes to any four of these nine questions, you may well be suffering from a manic illness and should consult a qualified professional. If you have

---

*Patients who are doing these things often lack insight and may fail to perceive the risks, which can be clear to anyone who knows the patient well. This is why it is important to interview the patient's spouse or family about her symptoms.

only two or three symptoms, you may have a mild form of mania (*hypomania*) and should still seriously consider a checkup. It is important to emphasize that the manic patient is often unaware of these changes in himself, which are obvious to those around him. The situation is further complicated by the fact that many manic patients deny that they are experiencing any problems at all because they feel so good. In cases of manic illness where the patient is unable or unwilling to acknowledge that he is ill, it becomes particularly important for the family to urge him to seek professional help. The consequences of manic illness, as we will illustrate, can be as self-destructive as the behavior of the depressed patient.

Like the depressive patient, the patient possibly suffering from mania should not try to explain his unusual feelings by life events. Life sometimes goes exceedingly well, and people can find plausible reasons for believing that their remarkable happiness is rational. As in depression, in mania what looks like the cause of the reaction may be the result of the symptoms of the illness. The feelings of euphoria may be a response to good experiences but a manic overvaluation of life experiences.

It is easiest to understand the manic patient by thinking of mania as the flip side of depression. When in a manic state, the depressed patient no longer lacks interest in life but is transformed into exactly the opposite kind of person. The manic is interested in everything and is bubbling over with plans. Her sense of optimism sweeps all doubts aside, and she often impulsively pursues impossible, unrealistic goals.

The depressive's lack of self-esteem is replaced by a grandiose conviction of tremendous power and superhuman capacities. The manic patient usually feels on top of the world, although some are intensely hostile and irritable and engage in furious squabbles, alienating friends, business associates, and family. Many divorces occur when one partner has become manic and the other finds the change intolerable.

The manic seems to be having such a good time that sometimes it is difficult for people to consider him ill, especially when the illness is a variation of the illness that makes people depressed. The fact that the manic patient frequently does not believe he is sick and refuses treatment is particularly unfortunate because excellent medications, such as lithium, are available for manic-depression. Therefore, the family members or friends have the extra burden of talking the patient into treatment.

■ *Aaron Archer* had been an energetic, prosperous investment consultant. His partners began to notice that he was working much longer hours and coming up with many more ingenious and creative ideas about how to make money. Initially skeptical about some of Aaron's ideas, his partners gradually became convinced that he was an authentic business genius. He was sensationally successful at persuading others of the merits of his schemes. He was his own best salesman, showing a dazzling command of facts and figures, and unshakable confidence. However, his partners were taken aback when he told them of his plans for a half-billion-dollar chain of health resorts throughout the United States promoting a secret Russian treatment that would restore youth and sexual potency to older persons. Aaron produced detailed demographic projections to support his ideas.

Because of the enormous investment necessary, some of Aaron's partners asked for more details about the nature of the secret miracle treatment. Aaron was outraged by such questioning of his judgment, and during several very unpleasant scenes he uncharacteristically ranted and raved about their lack of support. Several of his partners gave in, but one insisted on seeing some proof that this was not some fly-by-night fad.

The partners were also somewhat disconcerted because the formerly staid, hard-working Aaron now seemed to have become a member of the jet set, with frequent flights to and from Europe in the company of attractive research assistants. His drinking had also increased substantially.

Financial and personal disaster finally struck when the partners discovered that there was no proof whatsoever of the usefulness of the new wonder treatment. Big investors refused to join the undertaking, and the company's large preliminary investment was irretrievably lost. Aaron quit the company, saying that he was surrounded by fools and assassins. His bewildered wife finally told him that perhaps he should get some help and received a storm of abuse for her well-meaning efforts.

Several months later Aaron became depressed. At first he attributed this to his loss of money, friends, and business. But eventually he became very inactive and quiet, interested in nothing and responsive to no one. He was finally hospitalized.

Treatment

Most of the patients we have described here are victims of biological depression, although in some of them the symptoms take the form of physical ailments, unusual behavior change, or substance abuse. For almost all of them, medication was very helpful, in some instances producing improvement when other forms of treatment had not done so previously. For patients whose depression is less severe or more clearly related to life circumstances, other treatments—primarily psychotherapy— or even the passage of time might serve as well. But the point we are emphasizing in this book is that for people who are incapacitated by biological depression treatment with medication should usually be the first choice. The excerpts that follow illustrate some of the recovery patterns that can occur with antidepressant medications.

■ *Jill Jason* finally became completely inactive. She didn't eat, she didn't sleep, and she didn't talk. On her doctor's advice her husband took her to a psychiatric ward in a general hospital. The hospital staff gave her a thorough physical examination and found nothing wrong except the effects of malnutrition. Jill thought that she was being punished for her sins. Her psychiatrist prescribed an antidepressant but warned her husband that often these drugs take three to four weeks to work.

During the first week Jill slept somewhat better and began to eat a little. During the second week she occasionally responded to her husband's questions or to comments about what was happening with the family.

On the seventeenth day of her treatment, when Jill's husband walked into her room he was astonished to see her sitting by the bed reading the newspaper. She gave him a big smile and asked how the children were. Jill's husband was flabbergasted. She almost looked like her old self. Jill said that it was like a curtain had been raised and that for the first time in months she could really feel and respond.

Over the next week her progress was astounding. She was the old Jill—laughing, optimistic, and full of plans to fix up the house. Her doctor warned them that she would have to continue on the medication for at least six months and that she would need regular checkups during this period.

■ *Mary Malloy*'s last boyfriend told her something must be wrong with her because she was constantly selling herself short. Further, he could not understand why somebody so attractive and intelligent wasn't getting anywhere. Mary had thought of herself as being attractive and intelligent when she was a teenager, but lately she had lost faith in herself. Finally, at the boyfriend's suggestion, she entered psychotherapy. However, after many months she hadn't improved.

Mary's therapist told her that her new low self-esteem and performance difficulties were due to fear of success. He suggested that her devoted parents had made an unconscious bargain with her: they would take care of her if only she would remain their little girl. Therefore, Mary must learn to become independent of her parents. When she had achieved independence, her depression would go away. These ideas seemed reasonable to Mary, although occasionally she thought that perhaps she was being dependent on her parents—and now on her therapist—because she was depressed, rather than the other way around.

After almost a year of therapy with no signs of change, Mary's parents told her that they would no longer pay her rent if she didn't switch from a psychotherapist to a psychiatrist. Mary discussed this with her therapist, who pointed to the possibility that again she might simply be heeding interfering parents and that perhaps she ought to give the psychotherapy more time. However, Mary was also getting somewhat discouraged with the psychotherapy since little seemed to be happening. She grudgingly agreed to a consultation with a psychiatrist.

The psychiatrist said that she thought Mary was depressed and would try giving her an antidepressant. She told Mary that there were several different sorts of antidepressants available and that if the first didn't work she shouldn't get discouraged. Initially the doctor prescribed the same sort of antidepressant that had been successful with Jill Jason. However, the medication gave Mary a dry mouth and constipation and didn't seem to help at all. She felt even more lethargic, and at times her thinking seemed muddled. She complained about this to the doctor, who told her that these medications often take four to six weeks to work and that she should stick with it. The doctor saw Mary regularly during the month to try to keep her courage up. However, Mary simply did not respond; if anything, she felt worse.

Mary's psychiatrist told her that it was too bad that the drug didn't work but that there was another whole group of drugs that often did work when the first did not. These drugs were somewhat of a nuisance to use because they required a special diet, and if the diet was broken, there was a chance of unpleasant or even dangerous side effects. This was bad news for Mary, who had already lost confidence in medication.

Her doctor was sympathetic and reassuring. In explaining all the pros and cons of the medication, she emphasized how Mary could benefit from it and pointed out that she couldn't continue the way she was.

Reluctantly Mary agreed, went on the diet, and took the new medicine. Although the doctor said the medicine might take several weeks to work, Mary began to feel somewhat more energetic within the first week. By the second week she had gone shopping and had bought herself some new clothes for the first time in three years. She also called her old friends.

By the third week Mary told the doctor that she might even have too much pep and that she was having difficulty sleeping. After the doctor adjusted the dosage of the medication, Mary soon simply felt good and active again. However, she had to see the doctor regularly to have her condition monitored and the dosage readjusted as necessary.

After six months Mary was working, had a new boyfriend, and was developing an interest in cooking. She was often the life of the party. Mary asked her doctor how long she had to be on the medication now that she felt perfectly well. Would she relapse? The doctor said that she couldn't answer that question. People with long-standing depressive illness often had recurrences when they went off medication. The only way to find out was to try. She said that since Mary had done so well for six months and her life seemed stable and rewarding, this seemed a good time to try.

However, Mary also wanted to know whether there would be any long-term serious side effects if she stayed on the medication for another six months. The doctor said that there would be no problem about continuing the medication for that length of time, and that they could make up their minds about discontinuing medication later. Mary was concerned because she was being considered for a promotion and she didn't want the possibility of a slump to interfere with her new career.

Mary's anxiety and panic attacks had also improved markedly. She was no longer worried that she might have a heart attack, but she was still anxious about the possible return of the feelings of panic. She was afraid that if she went off the medication they might come back.

■ *Milton Meyer* began to examine every aspect of his life carefully. He attributed his apathy to a midlife crisis, which he understood was fairly common among men his age as they recognized that their adult life was half over. He had read of existential psychotherapy, which addressed such issues, and after discussing it with a close friend who was a psychologist, he entered therapy.

In the process of self-examination he began to belittle his work as a surgeon and minimize his contributions. He viewed himself as someone who had been programmed by his family and background and had lived his life according to their schedule. He saw himself as living out his parents' wishes for themselves in regard to his choice of career, spouse, and lifestyle. He also began to feel, first from a philosophical standpoint and later from an emotional one, that life might not be worth living and that suicide deserved serious consideration—a rational response to an irrational existence.

At this juncture Milton's psychotherapist became worried and referred Milton to a psychiatrist with whom he sometimes worked. Because many of the psychotherapeutic interpretations had made sense to Milton, the psychiatrist had difficulty in convincing him that a major depression, of biological origin, might be playing a role in the evolution of his feelings. The psychiatrist wisely did not challenge Milton's intellectual stance, recognizing that he would rather abandon psychiatric treatment than give up his painfully acquired insights. When the psychiatrist queried Milton about his symptoms, he found many that had been unreported simply because Milton had not been asked about them by the psychologist, whose treatment focus had not been on depression as a possible disease. In addition to Milton's disproportionate self-criticism, suicidal thoughts, and a loss of interest in his usual pursuits, he had noticeable sleep problems, awakening frequently in the middle of the night and early in the morning, a decreased ability to concentrate, diminished sexual interest, and a characteristic fluctuation of his symptoms during the course of the day.

The psychiatrist finally persuaded Milton that medication might constitute a useful adjunctive treatment to help with the physiological problems (which Milton believed had come from his psychological ones) and that he should continue to work on his psychological ones in therapy. When tricyclic antidepressants were administered, Milton experienced improvement of his depression in the expected sequence. These first-generation antidepressants were the original antidepressants and are as effective as the "second-generation" or "new" antidepressants. Newer agents have fewer side effects, but are probably no more effective; in some patients, they may be less effective. In Milton's case, sleep problems diminished and had disappeared by two weeks, his energy and concentration slowly improved, by six weeks he was regaining his interest in surgery, the violin, and gardening, and in successive weeks he experienced increasing affection for his family, a return of his sex drive, and a marked lessening of his philosophical concerns. The psychiatrist suggested maintaining drug treatment, citing evidence that such depressions have a natural history that must be played out, and during that time medication usually suppresses symptoms. Milton gladly agreed and began to rethink his psychotherapeutic experience.

He continued to believe that he had experienced a midlife crisis and that it had been important for him to re-evaluate his life goals at that particular time. He also continued to believe that to some extent his parents' expectations had programmed him—as such expectations do for most people— but over time he considered this less important, recognizing that the only way not to program a child is to bring him up without human companionship on a desert island. When his medication was diminished and discontinued after a year and a half, Milton re-experienced a recurrent, slight, but identifiable loss of interest in his customary activities. He was placed on antidepressants again, and repeated attempts were made every few months to discontinue them. Five years later he continued to require maintenance doses of antidepressants in order to avoid recurrence of severe depression.

■ *Bob Bush* had now been to three gastroenterologists. He had had X-rays of his stomach and small and large intestines. Nothing had been found. The last doctor stated firmly that continued tests were going to be a waste of time and that even if the president had had a colonoscopy that didn't mean that Bob should have one.

However, the doctor had just read that antidepressants were often helpful for people with bowel complaints for which there didn't seem to be any physical cause. Bob said that he would go for anything if the doctor thought it might work.

Bob was started on medication and after several weeks his abdominal distress disappeared. He no longer felt he had to check out bathroom locations. His work improved, and he suddenly found that he was also enjoying life a great deal more. Looking back, he could see that he had been in a real slump without knowing it.

■ *Peggy Pearl* had refused to go to doctors several times, and her husband was getting fed up with her growing abuse of alcohol. He finally told her that unless she got help he was going to leave. Peggy replied that all her troubles were due to him but he shouldn't leave.

The Pearls agreed instead to see a marriage counselor. The counselor listened to their mutual complaints for several weeks and then told Peggy that he thought she needed something more than marriage counseling because she was drunk half the time. During this period her husband's resolve to leave unless she got adequate care had been strengthened by their discussions. Peggy also was becoming increasingly aware that everything was not her husband's fault and that she had an illness that was destroying their lives.

The marriage counselor recommended a psychiatrist to whom he had often referred patients. When Peggy saw the psychiatrist, he told her that she was clearly abusing alcohol but that he thought she was doing this as a result of the severe depression she had experienced before the excessive alcohol use began. He treated her with an antidepressant, and after several weeks Peggy's mood substantially improved and she found herself resorting to alcohol less. However, her mood was very variable, and she continued to have bad weeks. The doctor suggested that adding lithium to the first medication might help. When the combination was tried, Peggy's mood became quite stable.

With the improvement in Peggy's outlook, she and her husband were able to work together again in marriage counseling. They did have real differences about many aspects of their life together, but now they could begin to make useful compromises instead of simply giving up and heading rapidly toward divorce.

■ *Saul Schwartz* refused to take antidepressants. He said that he wasn't depressed, that he just had a backache. He also refused to see a psychiatrist because that was for crazy people. His doctor and the family talked to him many times but accomplished nothing. Finally, at the instigation of Saul's desperate family, the family doctor took a real risk and told Saul that he had a new medicine that was good for backs. Saul was not told that it was actually an antidepressant.

Since Saul was still a free citizen who was in complete charge of his own life, this was a violation of his civil liberties. Patients should not be forced or misled into taking medication against their will. Only if they go through a legal hearing and are declared incompetent by a court can their decisions be put aside. In some states even this is not enough and the courts demand a re-review of all such medication orders even if the patient has already been found incompetent. Thus, the paternalistic actions of Saul's doctor were highly risky. Even the agreement of Saul's family that the prescription of a misidentified medication was necessary would be an inadequate defense in a lawsuit.

Saul didn't like the new medication much because it gave him a dry mouth and constipation, and he wanted to stop taking it after a few days. However, his wife carried on so that he agreed to take the new pills just to have a little peace.

In a few weeks Saul became more active and started talking about going back to work. He also started to laugh for the first time in months. When asked if he was feeling better, he said he felt just the same as he always did, and that his only problem was his back, which seemed a little less bothersome. He still didn't understand why other people had ever called him depressed. He also didn't see why his wife kept insisting that he continue his medication.

■ *Ralph Rogers'* family was shocked to hear that their son was a drug abuser. They immediately took him to a psychotherapist, whom Ralph saw twice a week regularly for six months. During this time his grades didn't improve, and he was spending more time out late at night with questionable companions. When his parents complained to his psychotherapist, the therapist said that such direct contact between them and him was interfering with therapy. Ralph had to understand that the therapist was on his side and not simply an agent of the parents.

That sounded reasonable, but the situation wasn't getting any better. Ralph's uncle told the parents that he had heard that a lot of these drug problems could be treated with medicine.

Mr. and Mrs. Rogers reacted negatively to this suggestion. After all, Ralph's problem was with drugs in the first place, so wouldn't additional drugs just complicate the problem?

After a year Ralph refused to see the psychotherapist any longer, saying that it was boring and a waste of time. The therapist said that Ralph had quit because they were getting close to the source of his difficulties. Ralph's friends told him that it was about time that he quit seeing "that shrink" because all his troubles were due to his parents' puritanical attitudes anyway. Ralph's parents oscillated between trying to ignore his difficulties, in the vain hope that he would snap out of it, and erupting into harsh shouting. Ralph continued to spend large amounts of time out with his friends. It was unclear how he was getting money for the drugs since he wasn't working.

Since at the same time *Richard Rogers* had quit work in response to his own troubles, Mrs. Rogers was in despair at having two emotional cripples on her hands. She suggested psychotherapy for her husband, but Richard said that it hadn't helped Ralph, so why should he try? However, when the family physician insisted that medication would help, Richard started to take antidepressants. Within a month he was no longer depressed. He slept well, ate well, had a restored interest in sex, and looked forward to getting another job. He was still desperately worried about his son, but he wasn't depressed.

Armed with the knowledge that medication had helped him, Richard told his son that he would have to move out if he didn't go to a psychiatrist for medication. Ralph preferred to move out, and bummed around for a year. Finally, strung out and broke, he returned home, His parents insisted that he have a psychiatric evaluation, and eventually he was treated with the same medication that had helped his father. His mood improved in six weeks, and he became interested in returning to school. He still used a great deal of pot and associated with semidelinquent buddies. His former bright future now seemed unlikely. His parents felt that, if they had caught his depression earlier, his change in lifestyle and the wasted year might have been avoided.

■   When *George Gelb* began to participate in the experimental drug study at the Depression Clinic, the psychiatrist also met with him half an hour per week for nine weeks, the duration of the study. The first 15 minutes of each session were occupied by formal questioning and the filling out of forms. For the second 15 minutes, during which the therapist was silent most of the time, George would reflect aloud on his condition. During this nine weeks his sense of sadness and other symptoms gradually seemed to disappear, and he began to act in a problem-solving way. After he discussed the forthcoming separation with his daughter and she elected to stay with him, he contacted a lawyer. Rather than passively resigning, he began to contest the divorce. He also investigated alternative job opportunities.

After nine weeks George was rated as moderately improved, but he had turned his life around. In the study, however, it turned out that he had been on *placebo*. George then accepted the option of taking the experimental drug. But in four weeks, before the drug had time to act, he had completely recovered.

George's story illustrates several characteristics of depression. First, some patients get better on placebo; second, many patients get better with the passage of time; third, many patients get better with the opportunity to talk things out with a therapist. George had not been receiving formal psychotherapy, but he had vented his feelings with the physician, who was sympathetic even though he made no suggestions or interpretations and engaged in no other standard psychotherapeutic maneuvers. The therapist listened while George came to terms with himself and began to solve his realistic problems.

■   When a psychiatrist first saw *Carl Carr*, he was a down-cast young man who talked slowly while recounting his symptoms and brooding about his hand injury. He had lost interest in everything but his fiancée, and was extremely anxious, guilty, and preoccupied with thoughts of suicide. He was close to failing at school, because he could neither concentrate on nor remember what he was studying. He had lost 15 pounds, had no energy or sex drive, and although he fell asleep easily, after an hour he awoke and tossed and turned for the rest of the night. His diagnosis was biological depression, triggered by life events, which had persisted for a year and a half and had been unresponsive to psychotherapy.

Carl's symptoms were classic, the kind that would be pointed out to medical students as typical of biological depression. Nevertheless, because the previous therapist had avoided a medical consultation and antidepressants, Carl may have had one-and-a-half years of inadequate treatment and unnecessary suffering. When the psychiatrist now prescribed one of the newer antidepressants, Carl responded quickly. Within two weeks his sleep difficulty was gone, at four weeks his interest in school returned, and by the tenth week of antidepressant therapy he was functioning as well as he had before the accident. His grades moved from C's to A's, and he and his fiancée moved in together.

The psychiatrist expected that Carl would remain demoralized because of his permanent physical handicap, which prevented him from doing work he enjoyed very much, but he took care of his demoralization himself. Without prompting, he recounted multiple instances in his life when he had been stymied but by personal efforts had succeeded. One year later, with minimal psychotherapy, he is functioning well, and the dose of medication is being reduced to see if his depression has disappeared. He is planning to get married soon and fully enjoys life.

■ Ten years late, *Edith Ebel* recognized her symptoms in a research advertisement for depressed subjects. In the study, she was first treated with an experimental drug, which worked. As the depressive symptoms responded, Edith became more interested in her job, her house, her golf, and her sex life. She worried less about trivia and suddenly realized that even her mind was working better—she had not previously noticed that she had been reading less and getting less out of it. The most surprising feature of her response to the antidepressants was the gradual withering away of her neurotic symptoms. She became less concerned with one-upmanship, she no longer felt the need to be a star, she became more gregarious, and her barbed hostility disappeared.

Edith has now been receiving antidepressants for three years. When they are gradually lowered or stopped, she does not suffer a full recurrence of depression but her personality reverts to what it was like in her predepression period.

Apparently a chronic mild depression increased Edith's neurotic response to her disturbing family. An awareness of the origin of some of her personality traits did not help her, but medical relief from the depression seems to have allowed her to change and grow in ways she could not before. In an autobiographical account she describes herself as now "knowing where I want to direct my life ... I am much kinder now ... I no longer rely on degrading peers. I now like myself and am very secure in who I am ... I believe that this attitude has resulted from my growing in wisdom and maturity ... My family agrees wholeheartedly and enjoys living with me."

■ *Aaron Archer* responded very well to the antidepressants that were given to him in the hospital. His ability to experience pleasure returned and he began to show interest in his former activities. However, he told his wife and doctor that he had a brilliant idea that would bring back his lost fortune. He refused to believe that he had been sick before his depression and viewed his mania as simply the way he was when he was normal. Finally, to placate his wife, he accepted the psychiatrist's suggestion that he go on lithium. His mood now shifted to normal. He was able to realize that his grandiose goals were indeed unrealistic and that his feelings of constant exhilaration had themselves been symptoms of an illness.

Mild Forms of Depression and Manic-Depression (Bipolar Disorder)

Depression and manic-depression are not like illnesses that are either present or not present. If one has tuberculosis bacteria growing actively in one's lungs, one has "pulmonary" (lung) tuberculosis. Without such bacteria one does not have pulmonary tuberculosis. If an artery in one's brain is closed by a clot and the part of the brain nourished by that artery's blood dies, one has a stroke. If the artery remains open, one does not have a stroke. But there are many other diseases that are not "all or none," black or white.

This is clearly illustrated in the case of weight. Some insurance company tables may state, for example, that a man of a particular body build, age, and height should weigh between 165 and 185 pounds. This obviously does not mean that if he weighs 164 pounds he is skinny or that if he weighs 186 pounds he is fat. Definite lines have to be drawn for purposes of categorizing people, but failure to maintain a weight between such a minimum and maximum does not necessarily reflect the presence of an underlying disease. Another medically important example is hypertension. As blood pulses in the arteries, driven by the heart, the pressure rises to a maximum, called the "systolic pressure," and declines to a minimum, called the "diastolic pressure." For young or middle-aged people systolic blood pressures over 140 are considered high and diastolic pressures over 90 are considered high. If one takes these numbers literally, a patient with a systolic blood pressure of 141 and diastolic pressure of 91 is "hypertensive." While someone with a systolic pressure of 139 and a diastolic blood pressure of 89 is considered to have normal blood pressure. The blood pressures of the two individuals differ by only 2 points, but one is considered sick and the other well. Obviously, this is a somewhat artificial framework.

The same situation exists with respect to depression and manic-depression. There are mild forms of depression called *dysthymia* and mild forms of manic-depression (bipolar disorder) called *cyclothymic personality*.

A psychiatrist does not decide if a depression is biological simply on the basis of severity. A person may be profoundly depressed for a while because of the loss of a loved one, and usually such a depression is psychological. On the other hand, some people have milder forms of depression that are biological in origin. The biological cause is discovered only when the depression disappears during medical treatment. Many of these people, who continue to lose interest and pleasure in life, and experience a decreased effectiveness in accomplishing daily tasks, frequently have a biological disease. Probably more than any single symptom, impairment in carrying out the responsibilities of one's life (as spouse, parent, homemaker, wage earner) raises the very real possibility of a biological depression.

Dysthymia

Many people have a prolonged, even lifelong form of mild, chronic depression, which is called "dysthymia." Below is a self-rating scale for dysthymia. We emphasize that what makes the difference between dysthymia and ordinary unhappiness is the chronicity and persistence of the symptoms. Even successes and satisfactions alleviate the enduring gloom only temporarily.

Self-Rating Scale for Dysthymia

A. Have you been depressed, sad, down, low, or blue for most of the day, for more days than not, for at least two years? (Or have others perceived you as being this way?)   No   Yes

B. While depressed do you have any of the symptoms in the Depression Self-Rating Scale at the beginning of the chapter?   No   Yes

C. 1. Do you have feelings of hopelessness or despair?   No   Yes

   2. Do you have pessimistic thoughts about the future, do you brood about past events, or do you feel sorry for yourself?   No   Yes

   3. Are you increasingly irritable or do you become angry more readily?   No   Yes

   4. Do you have recurring thoughts of death or suicide?   No   Yes

D. Have the past two years gone by without as much as two months of good feelings?   No   Yes

If the answers to A and D are Yes, and if you have had any of the symptoms in B and C, you very possibly have a dysthymic disorder and should receive an evaluation by a psychiatrist. Persons exhibiting this kind of depression used to be called "neurotic," implying incorrectly that their depression stemmed from psychological causes and that a cure for their depression would also have to be psychological, in the sense of psychotherapeutic.

A typical case history follows:

■ *Harry Hall* and *Bill Bagley* became friends in high school. Neither was particularly handsome, athletic, popular, or well liked, but they were not considered offensive and were not rejected by their classmates. They shared an interest in fixing old automobiles and spent many afternoons tinkering with an old Ford. In their working-class families money was always in short supply. Neither boy saw any opportunity to go to college. After high school they obtained blue-collar jobs in the same factory, which offered little chance for advancement. Harry complained a great deal about his unrewarding life, the lack of social and sexual opportunities, and his perpetual feelings of fatigue and boredom. Bill shared many of these complaints, and although he was more outgoing and energetic, he was also realistically pessimistic and resigned to his life.

When the United States entered the Vietnam War, their factory suddenly experienced a huge demand for its products. Even workers with only moderate experience were given the opportunity for rapid advancement. Harry saw this as yet another burden since he did not believe he could improve his skills sufficiently to rise to a higher level. Bill, on the other hand, seized the opportunity by going to night school and by requesting further on-the-job training. He was quickly promoted and, shortly thereafter, saw his life improve in another respect when he fell in love with an attractive and lively girl who reciprocated his feelings.

When Harry's reliable on-the-job performance was recognized, he too received a substantial promotion, but his gloom persisted. The more responsible job required him to supervise the work of men under him, which he found very difficult. Harry eventually did find a girlfriend, and once she knew him better, she pointed out that his gloominess and lack of pleasure were out of keeping with the realities of his life. By now he was being paid fairly well, had the opportunity for further advancements, was having a pleasant, if not exactly passionate, relationship with his girlfriend, and could pursue his hobbies more easily. Nonetheless, he remained downcast, tired easily, and was often bored.

A physician's checkup showed nothing particularly wrong, but in response to his girlfriend's urging, Harry told his physician that he just wasn't enjoying life the way he should be. The physician recognized that Harry's complaints were best understood as a mild, chronic depression and prescribed a new antidepressant that had been strongly recommended as low in side effects and broadly useful. Harry reluctantly agreed to try the medication. To his surprise, after about a month his girlfriend pointed out that he seemed more energetic and decisive, and that his habit of chronic complaining had largely ceased. Harry had not noticed any change.

These gains were maintained for the six months that Harry stayed on the medication. Then, with his doctor's approval, he decided to stop taking it to see what would happen. Life was going much better and he was feeling pretty good, so maybe the medicine was by now superfluous.

Unfortunately, after Harry had been off the medication for three months, his girlfriend noticed that he was losing interest and drive and was starting to complain again.

Bill and Harry had seemed much the same in early life. Both felt pessimistic—they believed they were unlikely to lead gratifying lives. However, given an opportunity, Bill was able to improve his life and experience real happiness. Bill, in other words, was suffering from chronic but realistic unhappiness and was able to overcome it by making good use of changing circumstances.

Harry, on the other hand, had chronic dysthymia. His illness was not obvious until his circumstances had improved enough to reveal the real discrepancy between how he felt and the realities of his life. Harry's dysthymia responded to medication, but as with many chronic illnesses, the medication did not cure his condition. When he stopped taking the medicine, the illness manifested itself again. Continuing medication is necessary for Harry to function at a normal level.

Might Harry have done well with psychotherapy? Is it possible that psychotherapy would have so changed him that his gains would have been permanent? We think not and will discuss this in detail in our sections on psychotherapy.

Cyclothymia

The milder form of manic-depressive illness, *cyclothymia*, is characterized by continual mood swings. The ups and downs last from weeks to months but never develop into a full-fledged manic-depressive illness. The answers to the two following critical questions can indicate whether or not you or someone you know might be suffering from cyclothymia.

A. Have you had a period of at least two years of fluctuating mood swings, with highs whose symptoms are listed under our section on mania and lows whose symptoms are listed under dysthymia?

B. During the two-year period with such mood shifts, have you been markedly impaired?

If the answer to A is Yes and to B is No, quite probably you suffer from cyclothymia and should obtain a professional evaluation. Cyclothymia shares one important feature with mania. During the up periods of cyclothymia, the individual is apt to think there is nothing wrong with him. He feels terrific, and if he has not suffered from the consequences of his illness (rash financial, personal, or vocational moves), he may actively wish not to have psychiatric help. Nonetheless, if you are a significant other in such an individual's life, and you clearly see these cyclothymic symptoms, you should as diplomatically as possible try to get him to professional care.

An illustrative case history follows.

■   *Walt Waverley* had known since early adolescence that he would be a writer. He found his greatest pleasure in turning his acute observations into vivid stories. He kept a diary and notebooks in which he jotted down odd turns of events and wry comments. During high school he was the star of his English class and the Creative Writing Club. At times his energy was remarkable, and he would spend all night writing a flood of stories, poems, and essays. He also had a lively social life, so much so that he was involved in a few drunken brawls and he was called in by the principal for a dressing down, a warning, and a period of probation. Walt was also very popular with girls, who found him vivacious, amusing, and ardent.

In his senior year, Walt slowed down noticeably. The flow of inspiration and humor dried up so that he spent long hours at his desk vacantly staring at a piece of paper. He began to eat and sleep more. Although he would respond to his partying friends, he was not the same old Walt. His school work suffered, and his friends told him that he was becoming a hermit. He said that the last year of high school was a drag.

However, after a dull summer, when he entered college in the fall he went back to writing with his old flair and energy. Once again he was successful, ebullient, and witty. He didn't understand what had happened to him over the past several months but attributed his returned energy to the stimulation of college.

Unfortunately, these periods of mood alteration became a routine part of his life. For several months he would be energetic and productive, and then for several weeks to several months his energy would flag, he slept and ate more, and he lacked his creative spark. He was never severely incapacitated during his depressed periods, but he tended to be apathetic and could not be productive. During his up periods, he was strikingly creative, although at times his rush of thought was so great that his output lacked clear structure. He also tended to drink and party too much.

Walt began to refer to his down periods as "writer's block." He began to see a psychotherapist, who attempted to get him to see his unproductive periods as the result of fear of success and as ways of punishing himself. Although eager to believe anything that would explain his inexplicable oscillations, Walt found the treatment ineffective. His therapist admitted that perhaps they weren't making much progress, and if Walt wished, he would be referred to a psychiatrist that he collaborated with on difficult cases. After much discussion, Walt eventually tried lithium. However, Walt was paying for both the psychotherapist and the psychiatrist and, therefore, limited the frequency of his psychiatric visits. When he developed side effects such as dry mouth, tremor, and frequent urination, the psychiatrist suggested that Walt be seen more often, so that dosage adjustment and blood-level monitoring could be carried out more effectively. The psychiatrist felt that it would require fairly close attention to find a dosage level that would even out Walt's mood without causing unpleasant side effects.

At this point, Walt discontinued the medication because he was afraid of it, felt that he could not afford closer monitoring, and feared that the lithium might interfere with his creativity. His psychotherapist supported him in this decision, saying that he was glad that Walt was mature enough not to look for a magical pill. Walt never took lithium long enough to find out whether it would work or if it would cause the feared decrease in productivity.

Although Walt's work was beginning to receive some recognition, editors found it difficult to develop a working relationship with him because his output was so erratic. His unpredictability was often blamed on his drinking, although interestingly his drinking occurred primarily when he was up rather than down.

People with cyclothymia often do not realize how their swinging moods dominate their life. They find external reasons for both the good and the bad periods. Most cyclothymic people never enter treatment, so this is not a well-studied group. We do know that at times cyclothymic mood disorder will turn into a full-blown manic-depressive disorder. We know this because, when careful histories are taken of manic-depressive persons concerning their life before the severe illness occurred, it often becomes plain that they had undergone a clear series of moderate ups and downs for many years that had gone unnoticed and untreated.

The Interpersonal Consequences of Depression and Manic-Depression

Depression and manic-depression affect not only the individual sufferer but all the people with whom he or she is involved—friends, relatives, employers. Some of the consequences of depression are relatively straightforward and easy to understand: to the spouse of the depressed individual, he or she is often a wet blanket. The depressive mopes, is uninterested in social activities or hobbies, is indecisive, derives little pleasure from anything, and is frequently irritable and angry. Well-intentioned suggestions that the depressed person should "buck up" or "snap out of it" not only are unsuccessful but are likely to provoke further annoyance and anger. Persistent recurrent depression can obviously be very hard on relationships.

Life with the manic-depressive individual can be intolerable in different ways. Excessive high spirits during euphoric mania, unwarranted by the circumstances of the couple's lives, are usually upsetting to the unaffected partner, who realizes that real-life problems and difficulties are being minimized, underestimated, and viewed through rose-colored glasses. If the mania takes the form of marked irritability, the relationship can begin to fall apart. The manic's impulsivity may also generate fear and anger. Spending sprees or poorly considered business initiatives may threaten the family finances or even bankrupt them. The increased sexual drive may disturb the partner, but what is far more likely to be disturbing and massively destructive is the manic's tendency to initiate casual sexual liaisons.

A spouse's depression can be withstood out of guilt and concern. However, the manic seems reprehensible because he is breaking the social contract while apparently having a wonderful time. Divorce frequently ensues.

With these examples of the kinds of problems that depressed and manic people can have, and of the good responses that many such patients have to medication, we hope we have conveyed some sense of the nature of these mood disorders. In the rest of the book we will go into more detail about the course of depression and manic-depression, theories about the causes of mood disorders, diagnosis and treatment, related disorders, and ways to get help. In particular, we will discuss the eventual outcome of Mary Malloy, Jill Jason, and Jane Harris to illustrate the wide range of possible outcomes.

3

What Happens to the Depressive or Manic-Depressive Individual Over Time?

BEFORE DISCUSSING the course of depression and manic-depression (bipolar disorder), we want to comment on the frequency of these illnesses. For reasons that are incompletely understood, depression has become increasingly common in recent times. That is, the rates of depression were lower for people born in 1900 than for those born in 1920, and lower for the 1920 group than for those born in 1940.

Recent figures are largely derived from a survey known as the Epidemiologic Catchment Area Program. This program used a specific interview to gather the data but did not use trained clinicians. Therefore, the figures can be considered only approximate. Almost 30 percent of the population reported a period lasting at least two weeks when they felt sad or blue. However, about 5 percent of the population reported a major severe depression during their lifetime. Dysthymia occurred in about 3 percent of the population, and another 3 percent of the population reported manic symptoms in the form of one-week periods or more of elevated, expansive, or irritable mood. Roughly 1.5 percent had a diagnosis of bipolar (manic-depressive) disorder. In any given year, 4 or 5 percent of adults became depressed. (The study did not evaluate people under the age of 18.) Therefore, roughly 10 to 12 million Americans become depressed each year, although not for the first time, and about 2 million have manic-depressive episodes each year. More recent epidemiological studies suggest that the numbers are even larger.

Depression is twice as common in women as in men, while manic-depression is equally common in both sexes. Although the reasons for this distribution are unknown, one popular theory is that women are more likely to suffer from depression than men because their lives are more oppressive. But is the rate of depression higher among groups of people who are disadvantaged, deprived, the targets of prejudice, or some combination of these factors? One such group is African Americans. When the rate of depression in this group was measured, the findings were unexpected. In blacks between the ages of 30 and 64, the rate of depression is slightly lower than it is in whites. This suggests that the relationship between social oppression and deprivation and depressive illness is not a clear-cut one. Attempting to explain the increased depression rate in women as due to "stress" also falters. If stress causes women to be depressed, and if stress shortens lives, why is it that women live significantly longer than men? The point is that it is easy to come up with psychological explanations when the real causes may be biological. We agree that discrimination and oppression are harmful, but this is very different from saying they cause severe mental *illness*. Despite the plausibility of such an explanation, it does not agree with the facts.

The gender distribution of severe depression may in fact be changing. For the past 45 years psychiatrists in Sweden have been studying a large semirural community, interviewing all of its members at fixed intervals to determine whether they have developed or are suffering from psychiatric illnesses. During the course of this study, the frequency of depression in young men has gone up tenfold.

Depression in young children and adolescents also may have increased. Up until the past ten years, psychiatrists believed that depression was relatively rare in adolescents and children. However, with growing evidence that some forms of depression are inherited, psychiatric researchers have begun to study the children of parents with these disorders, and they have found that symptoms of depression—usually but not always mild—can be identified in such children. Frequently, the depressions in children have not been recognized by the parents and are found only when the children are interviewed. Systematic studies on depression in children are now under way.

The Symptoms of Depression in Children and Adolescents

Although the major symptoms of depression in children include many of those seen in adults, other symptoms seem more specific to childhood—such as poor relations with parents, siblings, and school mates, irritability, and "insatiability." Many parents report that it is impossible to make these depressed children happy. This insatiability of depressed children corresponds to the loss of interest in life and the inability to enjoy oneself experienced by adult depressives. Depressed preadolescents, unlike many younger children, can report some subjective symptoms of depression—experiences of sadness, thoughts of death or suicide, and disturbances of sleep. Parental information on preadolescents is still useful, however, because parents are quicker to perceive symptoms that the child may fail to recognize, such as poor social functioning, irritable mood, and lack of interest in normal childhood activities.

Depressive disorder tends to develop slowly in younger children, but it is more likely to be relatively sudden in adolescents. In adolescents, the disease shares more of the symptoms of adult depressive disorder, such as feelings of inadequacy. The picture is complicated by the tendency of depressed youngsters to develop behavioral problems that involve rule violation or delinquent activities and to abuse alcohol and drugs. It is possible that in turning to such substances, depressed adolescents are unwittingly groping for "over-the-counter" antidepressants. We want to emphasize this because the substance-abuse problem may be the squeaky wheel that gets the psychiatric attention, while the accompanying mood disorder is being overlooked. Adolescent depression is also very changeable and may alternate with excited, exuberant periods.

A number of other childhood psychiatric disorders overlap with and may look similar to biological depression. If a child has symptoms suggestive of depression, he should receive a full evaluation from a child or adolescent psychiatrist.

In identifying depression in children and adolescents, it is important to know that, if depressive or manic-depressive disorder is present in one or both parents, the odds that the child will develop such an illness are considerably increased. Thus, if a parent(s) has mood disorders and her child or adolescent develops psychological problems of any kind, an evaluation is even more necessary than usual. Such early psychological problems may forecast a mood disorder, even though all of the symptoms may not appear at once.

Parents are unlikely to obtain psychiatric evaluations for their children for several reasons:

1. As noted, until recently, depression and manic-depression were thought to be exceedingly rare in preadolescent children. Similarly, it had long been believed that bipolar disorder did not occur in children. But recently, it has been claimed that many children with attention-deficit hyperactivity disorder actually suffer from bipolar disorder. Yet many of these children have chronic rather than periodic illnesses (bipolar disorder is characterized by periodic illness in adults) and there is no evidence that these children respond to antimanic drugs. There may be something seriously wrong in many of these children, but whether it is bipolar disorder is questionable.

2. Parents can seem to find reasons to "explain" their child's psychological or behavioral changes. Since all of us have experienced repeated frustrations and disappointments that can provide us with "reasons" that seem to explain our own

erratic moods, we apply these "reasons" to our children as well. However, we should be suspicious of our logic. Were someone, unbeknownst to you, to place a drug in your morning coffee that made you profoundly depressed, you would undoubtedly be able to find current and past life experiences that would seem to adequately explain your depression.
3. Parents are often unaware of the feelings of their children. In one study of children of depressed parents, one-third of the children were found to be depressed, a situation unrecognized by their parents.

Warning Signals for Parents

During preadolescence the hallmarks of depression are:

1. Inexplicable decrease in academic performance.
2. Increasing social isolation.
3. Loss of interest in sports.
4. Development of unusual physical complaints for no medically sound reason.
5. Increased childish and dependent behavior.
6. Excessive demandingness.

A childhood disturbance that closely resembles depression and that may turn into a depression in later life is extreme social anxiety. Such children are extremely shy, avoid social gatherings, become extremely anxious when called upon to perform in public, as in giving a report in class, fear authority, and cannot initiate social interactions.

In adolescence, the symptomatology of depression changes. However, since adolescence has gotten a bad reputation, parents are not always aware of what might be early warning signs of depression. For example, it is commonly believed that it is normal for an adolescent to go through extreme moodiness, outbursts of temper, and delinquent behavior. This is simply not true. Most adolescents living under reasonable and nondepriving circumstances do quite well. Therefore, one should suspect depression if one observes the following:

1. Marked moodiness.
2. Overreactions to frustrations out of all proportion to the provocation.
3. Marked self-isolation and social withdrawal.
4. Unrealistically low self-esteem.
5. Unwarranted belief that others dislike or reject him or her.
6. Unrealistic belief that one's personal appearance is ugly or offensive.
7. Loss of interest in hobbies, sports, and personal self-care.
8. Development of delinquent activities, in particular the abuse of drugs and alcohol.

One of the great problems in evaluating adolescents is that many teenagers use illegal drugs and alcohol. Thus, it is often not clear whether their use of these substances has induced a depression and then disrupted their lives, or whether the depression has caused the illegal drug use to begin with. Frequently, the only way to determine the cause of drug or alcohol abuse is to hospitalize the patient away from drugs and alcohol and monitor him for a period of abstinence. Unfortunately, such lengthy diagnostic hospitalizations are no longer possible with managed-care restrictions. If the drug abuse was due to depression, one would expect that the depression would persist or even get worse, whereas if the drug abuse or alcohol caused the depression, then one would expect that this would be alleviated by abstinence.

If you observe any of the behaviors discussed here, seek the advice of a child psychiatrist.

The "Natural History" of Depression and Manic-Depression

A medical description of the course or "natural history" of an illness is a description of its possible outcomes: how long it lasts, what proportion of patients get better or worse, and how quickly patients recover without treatment. The natural history of depression follows several common patterns, and in most of them the symptoms will likely return from time to time. However, these recurrent symptoms can usually be controlled. In the rest of this chapter, we discuss several courses of depressive illness and of manic-depression that we have observed in our patients.

Patterns of Depressive Illness

If we were to come up with a typical pattern for depression, it would look something like this:

Well → Depressive illness → Well

In this form a person is going along without any life problems—minding her own business, so to speak. Then, either in reaction to life difficulties or for no apparent reason, she becomes depressed.

These depressions usually last from about six months to two years. The number of such depressive episodes that a person can experience varies tremendously. Some people have only one attack of depressive illness, some people have several, and an unfortunate few suffer many attacks. The intervals between attacks also vary considerably. Sometimes episodes occur in bunches and do not recur for many years, while in other instances depressive episodes occur at widely spaced intervals.

■ *Jane Harris* was treated with Prozac, but showed little effect from it for approximately four weeks. Between four and six weeks, however, she started to develop her old interests, became energetic, and widened her social activities. Within ten weeks, she had returned to her former energetic, rewarding life. Her doctor warned her that she would require at least six months of treatment since there was a good chance of relapse if the treatment was stopped too soon. After six months, Jane did stop the medication and maintained her gains completely. She checked in with her doctor every few months over the ensuing year, and after that, they talked yearly. Jane and her doctor hope that there will never be a recurrence of her illness and they may be right, but there is no way to be sure.

Another pattern may look something like this:

Well → Depressive illness → Treatment →
Well → Treatment discontinuation →
Mild chronic depression

In this pattern a person who develops a depressive illness is treated with medication, after several weeks or months, the patient feels better, and the medication is diminished and then stopped. The person no longer experiences the symptoms of intense depressive illness, which was treated, but he or she does not feel up to par. For example, the patient's interest in his usual activities may not have completely returned, and he may still be rather passive, with decreased self-esteem and decreased energy. These are the symptoms of a new and persisting mild depressive illness.

These mild symptoms can be eliminated by the same medication that treated the severe depressive illness, but their control requires the continuing administration of the medication. In other words, the patient must continue to receive antidepressant medication regularly if he or she is not to suffer a relapse into the symptoms of mild depressive illness.

■ *Mary Malloy,* after a year of feeling well, was tired of staying on the diet her medication required. Her doctor told her that he was not sure what would happen when she went off medication but that he would follow her closely and they would see. After the medication was discontinued, Mary experienced two good months. She felt fine, her old self, and continued her outgoing pattern.

Slowly, insidiously, she began to sleep more and more. She found that on weekends she could sleep the day away and that it was progressively more difficult to get up for work. Because her weekends became disorganized, she found herself snacking on potato chips all day, often washed down with a beer or two or three. Her weight began to go up. Her relationship with her boyfriend became somewhat rocky when she started to complain that he was ignoring her, although in fact his behavior was no different than usual. Finally, she and her doctor agreed that things were not going well since the medication was stopped and that she was having a relapse. With the resumption of medication, the disease's process was interrupted, and within six weeks, Mary was back to normal.

She and her doctor discussed this in some detail. She pointed out to Mary that it was unfortunate that she had a chronic illness, but that she really had to look upon herself in exactly the same fashion as somebody with hypothyroidism who has to take thyroid supplements for the rest of his life, or somebody with diabetes who must take insulin to stay in balance. Nobody likes to be ill, but if you are ill, it's reassuring to know that there is a medication that effectively brings you back to normal. Furthermore, these medications do not lose effectiveness over time. In a year or so, they might try going off the medication again, although they shouldn't be overly optimistic about the outcome of this. Nonetheless, some depressive illnesses do seem to burn out with age and perhaps eventually Mary would not need medication.

■ *Jill Jason's* story was somewhat different. She too had done extremely well on medication, continued on it for six months, went back to work, and maintained her gains for three years. Then, abruptly, and for no apparent reason, her depression returned with full force. However, by then, Jill's husband knew the picture and forced her to go for treatment immediately, to which she once again responded.

Since this was her second episode of severe depression, her doctor discussed with Jill and her husband the possibility that she should receive a prophylactic medication—that is, that she should not go off medication at all but take medication daily in the hope that this would prevent recurrences.

Jill adamantly opposed this. After all, she had had several very good years and was there any assurance that her disease would recur? Therefore, once again after six months, the medication was discontinued. Jill went along perfectly well for five years, when she had another recurrence, which again responded to the hastily instituted treatment.

Jill's doctor was firmer this time, saying "Three episodes of severe depression is really too much. The odds that you are going to have another are high." Jill and her husband were left puzzled. The doctor assured them that there were several different medications that might be used for the prevention of recurrence and that they were safe, effective, and had little in the way of side effects, although they did require monitoring. What Jill and her husband had to balance was taking medication indefinitely versus the likelihood of repeated and marked life disruptions.

One important psychological factor was Jill's reluctance to be considered ill. Taking medication every day reminded her every day of her illness, and this upset her. Her doctor counseled the family over some time. Finally, Jill's husband told her that he couldn't see her go through another one of these episodes—for her sake, not just for his. At this point, Jill reluctantly agreed to take lithium. Even though she was not a manic-depressive but had recurrent unipolar depression, lithium was an effective treatment in the prevention of recurrent unipolar depression.

After two years on lithium, Jill complained to her husband that she felt that she was running out of gas. She did not have the severe insomnia, loss of appetite, and social withdrawal that she had previously, but nonetheless, there was a clear problem. Jill's doctor gave her an antidepressant in addition to the lithium, and she quickly returned to normal. It seems that, for many people, lithium may not entirely block depressive recurrences, but it does modify their severity so that the depression is not as painful and incapacitating and is more easily treated. Without lithium, Jill would undoubtedly have had yet another severe depression at this point.

A third pattern we have observed is the following:

Mild, chronic depression → Depressive illness →
Treatment → Well → Treatment
Discontinuation → Mild, chronic depression

In this pattern the patient has been mildly and chronically depressed from adolescence or even childhood, develops a depressive illness that is treated, and experiences a newfound feeling of well-being. When his medication is discontinued, he then returns to a state of mild depression. Interestingly, before they have the depressive illness, many of these patients do not know they had always suffered from depression. But when they develop depressive illness and are successfully treated with medication, they feel better than they have ever felt in their life. This is not because medication has made them high or manic. It is simply that when the symptoms are removed, patients notice the difference. Such patients are similar to a child with a vision defect who begins to wear glasses that successfully compensate for the defect. When such a child realizes that he now has no difficulty in figuring out what is on the blackboard, he begins to see himself differently. To be exact, we cannot say that depressed patients of this kind have been depressed since birth, but we can often say that they have been depressed as far back as they can remember; in many instances, this may be as early as five or six years of age.

One final pattern may look like this:

Well → Mild depression → Well → Mild depression → . . .

Not only severe depressive illness but also mild depression can occur in episodes. When mild depressions appear and disappear on an irregular basis, they are often not noticed or are mistaken for psychological depressions. We would like to reemphasize the point we made in chapter 2 that it is not severity that distinguishes a biological depressive illness from a nonbiological depression but the *pattern of symptoms*. The same persons who can experience severe episodes of depressive illness may at other times experience similar but less intense episodes of depression. Recognition of the nature of these illnesses is important because they frequently respond to medication and may not respond to psychotherapy. Certainly, if major depression is followed by a "minor depression" or dysthymia (chronic, mild depression), and psychotherapy has not been effective within three months, medication should be considered.

Patterns of Chronic Depression

Twenty or thirty years ago it was believed that when an episode of depression resolved the patient's mood returned to normal. This is frequently not the case. Current estimates are that approximately 20 to 25 percent of persons who suffer a biological depression will develop a mild, chronic depression, which in turn may be punctuated by episodes of severe depression. It is increasingly obvious that many such patients must remain on antidepressants permanently or semipermanently. They are like patients with pernicious anemia, whose symptoms can be relieved by the administration of vitamin B12 but who must stay on that vitamin in order to prevent the recurrence of pernicious anemia. Another analogy is that of epilepsy (which bears no relationship to depression). Many epileptics suffer seizures at infrequent intervals—for example, three or four times a year—but take an anticonvulsant on a continuing basis. A similar situation seems to hold for many depressives. As researchers in psychopharmacology have been able to follow their patients for longer periods of time, they have begun to recognize that chronic depression may be even more common than previously believed and may require indefinite antidepressant therapy.

Patterns of Bipolar Disorder

The course of bipolar disorder can be much more variable than the course of unipolar depressive illness, because any new episode can be either "up" (the manic phase of the illness) or "down" (the depressive phase). In addition, both "up" and "down" episodes can be either mild or severe. In other words, a manic-depressive patient may be manic, hypomanic (manic without impairment), mildly depressed, or severely depressed. An additional complication is that the onset of manic-depressive illness is unpredictable. The following two patterns illustrate how manic-depression can vary:

Well → Depression → Mild depression → Well → Depression → Mild depression → Manic → . . .

In this pattern an individual may experience several episodes of depression—separated by either complete recovery or mild depression—suffer several such bouts, and only much later have a manic episode. In effect, the patient has been manic-depressive, but the diagnosis could not be made until the first appearance of mania.

Here is another pattern of manic-depressive illness:

Normal → Mania → Normal → Depression → Normal → Depression → Normal → Depression → . . .

In this course a manic episode is followed by a return to normality, followed by recurrent depressive episodes with intervening periods of normality.

How often new episodes occur varies a great deal, from only one attack of manic illness in a lifetime to several per year. The major medications used in the treatment of manic-depression, lithium and certain anticonvulsants, can prevent attacks of mania or depression, or they can diminish the severity of attacks; when given for a long time, they may prevent attacks altogether. Studies have found that the average person with manic-depressive disorder loses about nine *years* from his or her life. That is, the person is unable to function as a student, homemaker, or worker for a total of nine years (usually spread out over a number of episodes). *Without treatment*, the average person with manic-depressive illness is out of commission for 9 of the 49 years between the ages of 21 and 70, or for about 18 percent of his or her adult life.

Patterns of Mild Manic-Depression

Some people have a manic-depressive illness in which they experience only mild forms of both symptom extremes. When they alternate in a fairly rhythmic and continuing way, they are diagnosed as "cyclothymic personality." Their "up" periods never exceed hypomania, so they do not become grossly impaired or require hospitalization. These ups and downs may follow each other without interruption, or they may be separated by normal intervals that can last for months. Such people are often referred to as "moody." Once one knows what to look for, the regular alternation of mood in this disorder makes it fairly easy to recognize. An occasional fortunate person is persistently hypomanic for much of his life without swings into depression. Such people are generally considered impressive, productive, creative people, and it is only the appearance of depression that makes it evident that their high productivity was to some degree the result of their disease-incited high level of drive.

4

What Causes Depression and Manic-Depression?

THE MAJORITY of cases of depressive and manic-depressive illness appear to be *genetically transmitted and chemically produced*. Stated differently, the disorders seem to be hereditary, and what is inherited is a tendency toward abnormal chemical functioning (sometimes called a "chemical imbalance") in the *brain*. Antidepressant medications apparently have a compensating effect, correcting the imbalances that are believed to cause depressive and manic-depressive illness.

Hereditary Factors: Patterns of Depressive and Manic-Depressive Illness in Families

Depression and manic-depressive illness—mood disorders—run in families. In the course of their lives, the brothers, sisters, parents, and children of a depressed person have a risk of approximately 20 to 25 percent of having the disease themselves. This contrasts sharply with the brothers and sisters, parents and children of a nondepressed person, 5 to 6 percent of whom may have the disorder. Although depressive and manic-depressive illnesses do occur more frequently in particular families than in the population at large, they do not always appear in the families we would predict they would and sometimes can skip generations. A grandparent may have one of the disorders, but his or her children may escape the disease or may have related problems with alcohol. Subsequently, the grandchildren may show symptoms of the illness. The type of depressive illness can also vary from one generation to another. It is not uncommon for a parent to be manic-depressive and for the child to have a depressive illness without the manic aspect. Finally, heredity does not seem to be an all-or-none matter. As we have discussed, depression and manic-depression occur in severe forms and in milder forms, such as dysthymia or cyclothymia. Close relatives of the depressive or manic-depressive may inherit either the severe forms or the mild forms of these mood disorders.

Heredity Versus Environment

The tendency of mood disorders of this kind to run in families has been recognized for hundreds of years. Certainly, the degree to which mood disorders occur in both parents and children does not tell us whether nature or nurture is more important. Are parents transmitting the illnesses to their children through their genes or by the environment in which they raise them? Might not being raised by a chronically depressed parent—one who took no joy in life or joy in his child's accomplishments, who because of self-preoccupation failed to praise his child and emotionally neglected him—produce depression in his child or even suicide? Suicide, which we discuss presently, also runs in families. But might not the willingness to kill oneself be learned? In certain cultures, such as that of Rome 2,000 years ago or of Japan as late as World War II, committing suicide was a socially approved way of avoiding a more horrible death, reclaiming one's besmirched honor, or sacrificing oneself for society's greater good. So the fact that suicide runs in families might simply be the result of a family member's experience with it. It is important to emphasize strongly that the degree to which depressive illness and manic-depressive illness occur in both parents and children does not tell us whether nature or nurture is more important. Some learned traits run overpoweringly in families—for example, with few exceptions the children of English-speaking parents speak English and the children of Russian-speaking parents speak Russian. On the other hand, some genetic traits appear in families inconsistently—for example, not all of the children of redheaded parents have red hair. Whether mood disorders are caused by heredity or environment—by nature or nurture—is of extreme importance.

Over the years geneticists studying psychiatric illnesses have tried to devise strategies to determine the extent to which depression may be inherited. One of the first methods used to tease apart the complex relationship between nature and nurture was the study of identical (monozygotic) and fraternal (dizygotic) twins. Identical twins arise from only one fertilized egg, which at an early stage in embryonic development splits in two. Fraternal twins arise from the fertilization of two different eggs. Identical twins (or identical triplets or quadruplets) are the only instances in which two individuals have exactly the same genes. The genes are the chemically coded instructions that oversee the development of the fetus and that miraculously enable a tiny fertilized egg to develop into the immense complexity of the human body and brain. Not only are identical twins very similar physically, but they are very similar mentally. For example, identical twins who have been adopted by different families in early childhood grow up with intelligence levels that differ from each other only slightly less than those for identical twins raised together. Fraternal twins are no more similar in intelligence than any other brothers or sisters in the same family.

Aware of such differences in the two kinds of twins, psychiatric geneticists decided to study psychiatric illnesses in identical and fraternal sets. The theory was very simply, if genetic factors played a crucial role in the development of psychiatric illness, then if one identical twin had the illness, his "co-twin" should have exactly the same illness. On the other hand, if a fraternal twin had such an illness, one could expect the co-twin to have the illness only about 10 percent of the time—the same rate as that for other brothers and sisters who were not twins. Identical and fraternal twins with psychiatric illness were observed in many settings, and it was repeatedly found that in about 33 to 70 percent of instances identical twins were "concordant" for psychiatric illness. That is, if one identical twin had a biological depression or a manic-depressive illness, then in about 33 to 70 percent of the cases the co-twin would have the disorder as well. The fraternal concordance rate was about 20 percent—slightly larger than anticipated.

Psychiatric researchers who believe that environment plays a large role reacted to these findings in two ways. First, they pointed out that many identical twins are raised in a special way: parents are likely to give them "cute" similar names (Barbara and Betty, Jane and June), dress them in identical clothes, and raise them so that they develop a closeness not seen in other siblings. Perhaps, it was reasoned, this accounted for the higher concordance rate in identical twins compared to fraternal twins. Furthermore, these theorists argued, if in 33 percent of "identical" twin pairs only one twin had the illness, then environmental factors—the psychological environment—must be playing a role. However, a study of identical twins raised apart in different families found that 8 of 12 sets or 67 percent were concordant. This is a percentage very similar to that of identical twins reared together and implies that similar upbringing is not the reason identical twins are concordant. In summary, this research strongly *suggests* that depression and manic-depression are genetic. However, the research cannot explain why "identical twins" are not really identical—completely concordant— 100 percent of the time.

It is useful here to compare this twin research with twin research on nonpsychiatric diseases. For example, the clearly biological disease of juvenile diabetes (diabetes in people under 30) has a concordance rate of only about 15 percent in identical twins. Club foot is an abnormality that involves genetic factors but is concordant in only 23 percent of identical twins (and much less, about 3 percent, in fraternal). In other words, for both psychiatric and nonpsychiatric illnesses, concordance rates in identical twins are variable. Identical genes do not always result in identical diseases. Depressive and manic-depressive illness, however, do appear to be more genetic in origin than some other nonpsychiatric biological illnesses.

The twin research thus implicated genetic factors but left the problem of the relative importance of heredity and environment unsolved. Identical twins of depressed parents might be depressed partially for genetic reasons and partially because of the psychological tendencies of twins to learn similar tastes, values, and ways of dealing with people and the world.

In the early 1960s, investigators took another step forward in distinguishing between the effects of nature and nurture when they hit upon the straightforward and simple technique of studying adopted persons. In adoptees one set of parents supplies the genes while the other supplies the environment. If it is true that psychiatric illness can be psychologically "caught" from a psychologically disturbed parent, early removal from that parent should prevent the later development of the disorder. But if the disorder is genetically passed from birth parents to child, the adopted child has just as great a risk of developing the illness in question as she would if she had not been removed from her biological parents. The adoption strategy has been applied to the study of several psychiatric illnesses, including depressive illness and manic-depression.

The adoption study of depression and manic-depression began by identifying one group of adults adopted in infancy who were now depressive or manic-depressive, and a comparison group of adoptees of the same age and sex who did not have depression or manic-depression. The investigators then evaluated the biological parents and siblings of both groups—*whom the adoptees had never met*—and the adopting parents who had raised them and the adopted siblings with whom they had been raised. If genetic factors play a role in the transmission of depression and manic-depression, then one would expect to see an increased frequency of depression and manic-depression in the biological parents and siblings of the adopted depressives in comparison to the biological relatives of the normal adoptees. On the other hand, if depression and manic-depression are transmitted by life experience and experience within the family, then one would expect to see a greater frequency of mood disorders in the adopting parents of the depressives and manic-depressives.

What was found? There was a greater frequency of mood disorders only among the *biological parents and siblings* of the adopted manic-depressives. This showed that genetic factors were playing a role. The other finding was that frequency of mood disorder among the adopting parents of the ill adoptees was not greater than that among the adopting parents of the psychologically healthy adoptees. In other words, no evidence was found that rearing played a role in the development of depression and manic-depression.

This study also had one unexpected and dramatic finding: the biological relatives of the mood-disordered adoptees were 15 times as likely to commit suicide as the relatives of the normal adoptees. How is this to be explained? It is highly unlikely that genes transmit a tendency to kill oneself. What is likely is that a mood disorder in these biological relatives resulted in their suicide (remember that from 10 to 30 percent of depressives and manic-depressives kill themselves). The same finding of genetic contributions to suicide was duplicated in a study in which investigators examined the biological and adopting relatives of adult adoptees who committed suicide and of a similar group of adoptees who had not. The suicide rate was 11 times as great in biological families of the adult adoptees who had committed suicide as it was in the biological families of the adult adoptees who had not committed suicide. Again, the plausible explanation is that the suicides of both the adoptees and their biological relatives, whom they had never met, were related to mood disorders.

Genes Plus Events Can Equal Depression

Many people have misconceptions about genetic illnesses. Even if an illness is genetic, that does *not* mean that other factors do not play a role in its development. A clear-cut medical example is juvenile diabetes. As we mentioned earlier, when an identical twin has juvenile diabetes, in only 15 percent of the cases does the co-twin also have the disease. Something other than genes is playing a role, and the chain of events is complicated. Apparently, individuals with a genetic tendency toward juvenile diabetes react abnormally to infection with a common virus. In these people the virus does not simply produce respiratory or gastrointestinal symptoms but seems to kill the cells in the pancreas that produce insulin; the result is diabetes. However, researchers still do not know why many co-twins do not develop diabetes, since presumably they have been exposed to the same virus.

Before discussing the roles of experience and biology, it will be helpful to clear up some old-fashioned and misleading terms. In the past, psychiatrists classified some kinds of depression as *reactive*—that is, produced by life events in a person who was predisposed because of a neurosis. *Neurosis* is a term that has just about disappeared from modern psychiatry. It was used to refer to psychological maladjustment that was thought to be the product of the patient's abnormal psychological structure, which in turn was thought to be the product of unfortunate life experiences. These reactive depressions were contrasted with *endogenous* depressions—that is, those depressions produced within the sufferer. An endogenous depression was believed to appear for no identifiable reason and was believed to be caused by abnormal biological functioning in the brain. Reactive depression was treated by and believed to be curable by psychotherapy. Endogenous depression was believed to be treatable, if at all, by physical methods, such as drugs and electroconvulsive treatment. So-called neurotic, reactive, and endogenous depression are labels that are beginning to disappear. One of the major reasons for their disappearance is the increasing evidence that *biological depression and manic-depression are often triggered by life events*, but nonetheless are treatable by physical methods.

As an example, let us consider people who appear to develop a severe depressive illness following the loss of a loved one or a major disappointment in life. Is the cause hereditary or psychological? The best evidence indicts both factors. Some people show a decreased psychological resilience, an inability to cope with stresses that most people can overcome. A similar medical situation exists in people who lack normal immunity to infection with bacteria and viruses. In our parents' generation, everyone was exposed to tuberculosis, but only 1 in 3,000 people died of it—people who for unknown reasons were unable to fight off the infection. All of us harbor bacteria within our mouths and our intestines, but we usually do not become ill from them. However, when immune defenses are lowered—either genetically (as in the well-known case of the little boy who had to live in a sterile tent) or by another disease (such as AIDS)—people do become ill from bacteria that do not bother others. Presumably, persons who manifest the symptoms of severe biological depression following a major loss have an analogous vulnerability—that is, they lack resistance to such experiences.

This *combination* of heredity and environment leading to disease is frequently seen in medicine. An example is a form of anemia seen in people of Mediterranean extraction. Many Mediterranean people inherit a tendency to develop anemia but do not show symptoms of that disease unless they eat broad beans or go to a part of the world where they must take a particular antimalarial drug. Otherwise, they may lead their entire lives without knowing they have a genetic disease. An example of a kind of depression with a similar pattern is "seasonal affective disorder." People with this disorder become depressed in the fall and feel better in the spring—apparently in response to the variation in hours of daylight. Seasonal depression clearly shows a mixture of hereditary and environmental effects; many of us become somewhat down during the darker months of the year, but few of us develop depressive illness.

Can Upbringing and Life Experience Cause Depressive Illness?

Many psychiatrists, both past and present, have believed that depression (the type was often unspecified) was produced by life experience and was best treated by psychotherapy. The first and most widely listened to proponent of this view was

Sigmund Freud, who began to theorize early in the twentieth century about the causes of mental illness. The psychoanalytic theories of depression have focused on unexpressed and unconscious (not perceived by the depressed individual) rage as a reaction to being helpless or dependent on others or to loss of a loved one. In such situations, it is argued, the patient cannot express his anger either because of fear of antagonizing the person on whom he is dependent, or because he does not want to recognize that the relationship with a deceased (or otherwise departed) person was not entirely positive. Presumably, in both instances, the unexpressed anger is kept in and bottled up, producing depressed feelings. In cases of loss that are accompanied by genuine mourning, what distinguishes depression from grief is that the component of anger is directed inward. Psychoanalytic attempts to determine the truth of such theories have been limited and inconclusive. Some investigators have suggested that abuse and neglect in early childhood can predispose to depression in later life. The information about abuse and neglect has come from reports by adults. There are great difficulties in evaluating retrospective evidence and this remains an unconfirmed theory. One new prospective study claims that childhood stress causes depression only in those with a particular genetic vulnerability.

Two major forms of psychotherapy, less intense psychological treatments than psychoanalysis, have advanced different theories of what causes depression. Two that are particularly popular at present are the cognitive-behavioral and interpersonal theories. The cognitive theory states that patients with depression have developed the depression because of errors in thinking—unrealistic attitudes about themselves and the world. The three major types of thinking "errors" are: (1) undervaluing oneself—low self-esteem stemming from the belief that one is inadequate and of little value; (2) a negative view of one's current experience—depressed people perceive themselves as unable to achieve their goals and unable to experience pleasure; (3) pessimism—the belief that things will not improve. A depressed person feels depressed because he is constantly putting himself down. Examples of such attitudes are: "I never get anything right," or "Every job has to be perfect or it's no good at all," or "Things will only get worse." These unrealistic expectations supposedly lead to a person's recurrent dissatisfaction with herself, which in turn leads to the feeling of depression. The job of the cognitive therapist is to convince the patient that there is no evidence for her self-defeating beliefs. The theory states that such persuasion will change the patient's distorted attitudes and help to lift her depression.

The interpersonal theory holds that the basic reason a person becomes depressed is that he does not know how to get along with his intimate partners. As a result he becomes increasingly disappointed and frustrated. The interpersonal therapist therefore focuses on the patient's key relationships. The therapist attempts to clarify how the patient behaves—for example, with his spouse or his children or his boss—and how the other persons, in turn, might be expected to react to his behavior. The theory proposes that when the patient begins to understand his effect on others, he can change his behavior and improve his relationships. This improvement in interpersonal relationships is supposed to rid the patient of depression.

Are these three theories correct in interpreting behavior and depression? Proving—or disproving—psychological theories is extremely difficult. Fortunately, we do not have to ask this question. We can ask the much simpler question of whether treatment based on these theories works and—it is a very big "and"—how does psychotherapy based on these theories compare with medication in the treatment of depression? Fortunately, an elaborate research study of the effect of these psychotherapies and of medicine on depression was conducted recently, under the sponsorship of the National Institute of Mental Health. This study was the first of its kind and very important, because the two psychotherapies were compared not only to each other but to a particular drug, imipramine (Tofranil), and to a placebo pill. Both the imipramine and the placebo were offered with medication-centered advice and reassurance—that is, a minimal "case-management" therapy.

What were the results? Unfortunately, the study received much misleading publicity. The early reports were that cognitive behavior therapy, interpersonal therapy, and drug treatment were all equally effective. A more careful look at the results by one of us (DFK) came up with a different answer: The outcome depended on whether the depression was mild or severe. In the mildly depressed patients, the drug, the placebo, and the two types of psychotherapy were all equally effective. The results were quite different in the more seriously depressed patients. For the severely depressed, medicine was better than both psychotherapies in terms of quickness, costs, and most important, degree of benefit. In the severely depressed patients interpersonal psychotherapy was somewhat more effective and cognitive behavior therapy slightly more effective than the treatment with the placebo. Furthermore, in patients with marked dysfunctional attitudes, interpersonal therapy was actually better than cognitive therapy. It remains possible that other forms of psychotherapy may work better than cognitive behavior therapy and interpersonal therapy, but they have not been studied as carefully, and available evidence is unpromising.

Although this study answered the question of how effective these two psychotherapies are, it did not answer the question of how effective the best drug treatment is. Only one drug was employed—imipramine—and it is the common experience of psychiatrists that many depressed patients who do not respond to treatment with imipramine do respond to treatment with other medications. The implication is that, if other drugs had been used in patients who did not respond to imipramine, the results would have been even more striking. A recent reanalysis indicated that many of these patients had an atypical depression marked by overeating or oversleeping. This subgroup did not respond to imipramine, but is known to show a high rate of response to monoamine oxidase inhibitors (MAOIs), which, however, were not used.

In light of the relative therapeutic ineffectiveness of these different psychotherapies, the theory that psychological factors produce depressive illness remains unsubstantiated.

Chemistry and Depression

The information that supports the view that depressive illness results from a chemical imbalance comes from studies of both

people and animals; currently, this body of work is being supported by new techniques, such as the PET (positron emission
tomography) scan, which can measure the degree of metabolic
activity in different brain regions. To provide some understanding of the results of these studies, we will describe in simple
terms the electrical and chemical functioning of the brain.

The brain is composed of perhaps ten billion (ten thousand
million) cells, each of which is connected to hundreds or thousands of other cells by thin strands called axons ("wires"). We
use the word "connected," but the axons do not actually touch
the other nerve cells; they are separated by very minute dis-
tances. Evolution has worked out a complicated method for
transferring signals from one nerve cell to another. When a nerve
cell is stimulated electrically or chemically, it sends an electrical impulse to the tip of the axon. This electrical impulse does
not stimulate the next nerve cell. Instead, the stimulated end of
the axon releases a chemical that crosses the brief gap and stimulates a second nerve cell. After it has stimulated that nerve cell,
most of the released chemical is picked up again by the axon
that had initially secreted it. In other words, the first nerve cell
acts like a sponge that releases fluid, stimulates the second cell,
and then expands and "sucks" the chemical back into itself.

These chemicals are referred to as *neurotransmitters* or
neuromodulators. There may be as many as 200 of them, and
many of them are located only in certain parts of the brain. This
means that if one injects an animal with a drug that is like a
neurotransmitter that functions only in one particular part of
the brain, the result is similar to placing electrodes in the nerve
cells of that part of the brain and stimulating it electrically. In
consequence, different chemicals can stimulate different parts
of the brain. For example, if activity of certain nerve cells stimulates an animal to become angry and fight, either electrical
stimulation of those nerve cells by wires or chemical stimulation that affects those nerve cells will make that animal angry.

The relevance for depression is that certain neurotransmitters are known to play a role in the regulation of mood. For
example, studies of the spinal fluid that bathes the brain show
decreased amounts of some neurotransmitters in depressed
persons. Three neurotransmitters seem particularly important

in depression: norepinephrine, dopamine (both very close chemical relatives of adrenalin), and serotonin. Antidepressant drugs have very specific effects on these three neurotransmitters. Some antidepressant drugs will prevent the cells that release norepinephrine from reabsorbing it. As a result, the norepinephrine remains in the small space between the axon and the second cell. What this does is unclear. It may cause the second cell to fire and to stimulate other cells at a greater rate. An alternative view is that the increase in the neurotransmitter actually turns *off* the second cell, and its antidepressant effects are due to a decrease in the functioning of hyperactive cells. Other antidepressants prevent the first cell from reabsorbing serotonin. The two most familiar antidepressants that do this are amitriptyline (Elavil) and fluoxetine (Prozac).

To use another analogy, antidepressant action seems related to the fact that the secreting cell maintains a "reservoir" of its own neurotransmitters and regulates the amount stored by breaking down excess amounts. Antidepressants such as tranylcypromine (Parnate) and phenelzine (Nardil) prevent the breakdown of surplus neurotransmitter; in essence, they seem to enlarge the reservoirs so that stimulation of the first cell releases larger amounts of neurotransmitter, causing greater stimulation of the second cell. The second cell's activities are due to stimulation of its receptors by the neurotransmitter. The analogy is often made between a key and a lock. The neurotransmitter is a particular sort of key that fits the receptor's particular sort of lock. However, this is too static a picture because we know that receptors can increase or decrease in number and sensitivity.

Unfortunately, theories about antidepressant function have some big holes in them. When antidepressants are given to animals, the effects discussed above are produced in the brain within minutes, or at most a few hours. But antidepressants take weeks to work in human beings. Perhaps the long-term administration of antidepressant drugs is required to increase the sensitivity of the second cell, so that normal amounts of neurotransmitter produce larger effects. All of this may require several weeks. At present, since this research is ongoing, we just don't have all the answers.

Norepinephrine, dopamine, and serotonin are not the only chemicals believed to play a role in the regulation of mood. Many other chemicals that affect its functioning have been found in the brain, and many more are believed to exist.

When the brain produces too little of any of these neurotransmitters, either naturally or because of the use of other chemicals, the body appears to deal with the problem by increasing the number of receptors—in that way the transmitters that are released have a better chance of taking effect. Examination of the brains of depressed persons who have died from other diseases reveals an *increased* number of some of these new receptors. The implication is that the body has responded to a failure to produce sufficient neurotransmitters by increasing the number of receptors.

The first well-established antidepressant, imipramine (Tofranil), has been shown to bind very tightly to the brain— just as brain chemicals known as endorphins do to endorphin receptors. This suggests that the brain may have its own imipramine-like chemicals. In fact, such chemicals may be the brain's own antidepressants! Another related observation is that the brains of depressed persons may have a decreased number of "locks" or receptor sites into which the imipramine can fit. A decreased number of receptors could produce decreased activity of these cells, which in turn could lead to depression.

Our understanding of all these matters still remains partial. One thing we do know is that drugs that make depressed people normal do not make normal people "high" or manic. They act like the thermostats in a house that turn on either the furnace or air conditioner depending on the temperature. Antidepressants lift the mood of the person who is depressed and lithium and other drugs "lower" the mood of the person who is "high."

The existence of different kinds of chemical abnormalities that may underlie depression gives us a clue as to why all depressed individuals do not respond to the same antidepressant. Psychiatrists routinely find that they may have to try several antidepressants before finding one that is effective for a particular individual.

In sum, although we know comparatively little about the altered chemistry of individuals with depression, our knowledge is advancing rapidly.

Other Illnesses and Depression

Physicians recognize that a large number of medical illnesses can cause depressive symptoms indistinguishable from those produced by imbalances in neurotransmitters. Among them are underactivity of the thyroid gland, mononucleosis, and hepatitis. The fact that medical illnesses can cause depression is another reason for requiring that a depressed patient have a full medical examination.

Some diseases are popularly believed to cause depression but do not. Two examples are hypoglycemia and allergies. Hypoglycemia is an uncommon disorder in which the amount of sugar in the blood drops to a subnormal level. When this occurs, the body tries to compensate—for example, by releasing adrenalin, which raises blood sugar and produces sweating, muscle tension, rapid heartbeat, and anxiety. There are distinct diseases associated with hypoglycemia, but they occur infrequently. The misdiagnosis of hypoglycemia as the culprit responsible for other diseases (such as depression) is now common; hypoglycemia is hardly ever the cause of depressive illness.

Another *supposed* cause of depression is an allergic reaction to food or to *common* environmental chemicals. There is no evidence that serious depressive illness is ever produced by such allergies. Unfortunately, considerable time and money are sometimes wasted pursuing these frequently indicted but unsubstantiated claims.

Predicting Depressive Illness

Physicians do not know the chances that any one child will develop depression, but it has been found, for example, that about 25 percent of the *daughters* of mothers with depressive illness will develop depressive illness themselves. This is obviously distressing, but an awareness of a genetic tendency helps a concerned parent or the vulnerable individual to detect the illness when it is beginning to develop. Early detection can mean early appropriate treatment. The depressed child, adolescent, or young adult may be spared unnecessary pain and the sometimes cumulative and far-reaching difficulties that stem from depressive illness.

We want to repeat that depressive illness and manic-depression do not necessarily follow simple genetic patterns: parents with one form of the disorder may have offspring with another. Depressive illness may skip generations. Both mild and moderate forms of depressive illness can be genetically transmitted, and the milder forms, because of their decreased severity, are frequently misdiagnosed as psychological in origin and incorrectly treated.

Remember, if there is depressive illness or manic-depression in the family, and if a close relative becomes depressed, or if he or she develops *any* severe or unexplained psychological symptoms (for example, anxiety attacks, withdrawal, or drug abuse), it is wisest and safest to assume that he or she may have a depressive illness and to obtain a psychiatric evaluation. Depression in preadolescents and adolescents may have different symptoms from those seen in adults—for example, problem behaviors of various kinds. Therefore, any long-lasting psychological symptoms deserve careful evaluation.

5

Diagnosis and Treatment of Depression

Diagnosis

WE HOPE in the preceding pages we have conveyed to you how important it is to obtain an accurate diagnosis prior to treatment of depression and related illnesses. Accurate diagnosis requires both a general medical and a specialized psychiatric examination. Although most patients with depression do not have another underlying medical condition, the possibility is great enough so that an initial evaluation must include appropriate medical screening. The physical examination should include the usual blood, urine, and other laboratory tests for the most frequent abnormalities associated with depression—such as underactivity of the thyroid gland—and the physician should also be aware of uncommon, but not rare, conditions associated with depression, such as hepatitis. If the doctor suspects that one of these less common medical conditions may underlie the depression, further medical examination is indicated.

It is good practice for patients with mild depression as well as those with severe depression to receive a medical evaluation.

There is no simple relationship between severity and the determination of whether or not a depression is biological. Most severe depressions are biological, but people who are undergoing great personal stress (grief, rejection, loss, etc.) may have severe symptoms. On the other hand, some mild, chronic depressions—which may seem to be produced by life events—are associated with widespread loss of interest and pleasure (anhedonia) and are primarily biological in origin.

In the psychiatric part of the evaluation, the psychiatrist will inquire about definite signs and symptoms characteristic of depression and other psychiatric conditions. (*Symptoms* are what the patient experiences. *Signs* are what someone else may observe, such as weight loss or trembling.) Like the internist, the psychiatrist inquires about both the presence and absence of symptoms. For example, the presence of apathy indicates depression, and the absence of delusions and hallucinations helps to rule out psychosis. The diagnostician will also be interested in the patient's life and problems before the present depression, and in the effects of previous treatments. She often wishes to interview family members to gain their perspective on the patient's difficulties.

Because depressive illnesses often run in families, the psychiatrist will want to know about the pattern of psychiatric illness within the patient's family. A relative's illness may provide a clue to the diagnosis of a patient whose current illness is unclear.

The process of sorting out symptoms, signs, and history to reach a diagnosis, a procedure called *differential diagnosis*, is essential for proper care. Effective treatments for one kind of depression may be ineffective for another and possibly even harmful for a third.

The first major question for the diagnostician is whether the patient has a biochemical depression or a psychological one. Answering this question requires great skill. Biological depression can be mild and respond to medication, while a psychologically caused depression may be more severe and yet respond better to psychological therapy. If the diagnosis is biological depression, the diagnostician can often recognize particular forms of the disease that respond better to one type of antidepressant medication than to another.

The psychiatrists who are best qualified to make this diagnosis have been well trained in modern biological psychiatry. However, as we mentioned earlier, many other physicians, such as internists and family practitioners, diagnose and treat depression. Unfortunately, many have not had the training necessary (1) to distinguish between biological and psychological depression, (2) to determine whether a patient has benefited as much as possible, nor (3) to use combinations of drugs in patients who initially obtain only partial relief from their symptoms. Indeed, this is still true of some psychiatrists. Similarly, many well-trained psychologists and social workers are skilled in the treatment of psychologically produced depressions but have not been taught to distinguish between biological and psychological depressions. One's best chance of getting an accurate diagnosis, therefore, will be from a psychiatrist well trained in the new biopsychiatry, sometimes called a psychopharmacologist.

After thorough diagnosis the psychiatrist can make predictions about the usefulness of pharmacological (drug) treatment, psychological treatment, or the combination of the two.

The Effectiveness of
Medical Treatment of Depression

In the previous chapter we discussed the effectiveness of psychotherapy in more serious depression. How effective are the medical treatments now available? Biological treatments for depression are dramatically effective. Eighty percent, or even more, of individuals suffering a major depression will respond to one or another of the antidepressant drugs, singly or in combination. Of the 20 percent of individuals with major depression who do not improve when given medication, many will respond to electroconvulsive therapy. There have been few pharmacological studies of dysthymia (mild, chronic depression), but it appears that this condition usually responds to the same antidepressants used to treat more serious biological depression. Unfortunately,

very little is known about the appropriate treatment of cyclothymia (mild manic-depression) since such patients are comparatively rare and no research programs have been directed
specifically at this particular illness. Since medication clearly is
beneficial for manic-depressive disease, it is likely that it would
help cyclothymia.

The Decision to Use Drugs, Psychotherapy, or Both: Relative Costs and Benefits

By his initial evaluation the psychiatrist can predict the likelihood of a given patient's depression being biological, and if so,
the likelihood of his responding to particular medications. As in
the rest of medicine, perfect certainty is not possible. The facts
he uses are these: Between 70 and 80 percent of people with biological depression will obtain substantial relief from medication.
This is true of mild as well as more severe biological depression,
whether it has begun recently or has been present for a long time.
There is only slight evidence that specific psychotherapies are
more effective than brief consultations with a physician who follows no specific psychotherapeutic approach. In a recent study
of the effects of psychotherapy and medication on depression,
conducted under the sponsorship of the National Institute of
Mental Health, practically no differences were found between
cognitive therapy and interpersonal therapy. Both showed only
slight superiority to the placebo treatment that included minimum support. We interpret these findings to mean that psychotherapy plays a role in treatment because its offers a very
believable and understandable form of support that is comfort-
ing to the demoralized and suffering patients, but that it is not
actually treating the underlying depression.

Should drug treatment or psychotherapy be tried first? A
good way of answering this question is to evaluate the advantages and disadvantages of four possibilities:

1. The patient is treated only with drugs. Her depression
   turns out to be biologically caused, so this is the appropriate treatment.

2. The patient is treated only with psychotherapy. His depression turns out to be biologically caused, so he may waste considerable time and money.
3. The patient is treated only with drugs, but his depression turns out be psychologically produced. The treatment is incorrect. However, this will be determined cheaply and fairly rapidly (usually within two to three months; if the patient is part of new drug trials, these rarely extend as long as six months).
4. The patient is treated only with psychotherapy. Her depression turns out be psychological in origin, so the treatment is appropriate.

Another major question concerns patients in category 3, who do not have a biological depression but who receive drug treatment. All drugs produce side effects—rarely, severe ones. The risks involved in taking any of the major psychiatric drugs, used in therapeutic amounts with the recommended precautions, are probably much lower than the risks of taking penicillin.

Although treatment response is informative *if* the patient responds, it is not if he does not improve. If a long-standing condition improves after taking drugs, that tends to confirm both the diagnosis and the benefits of medication. However, there is some trial and error in drug prescription. Patients may respond to the second or third medication prescribed rather than the first.

Even failure to respond to all known biological treatments does not necessarily mean that the patient's problems are strictly psychological. It may simply mean that useful biological treatments have not yet been developed for her particular illness.

Similarly, failure to respond to psychotherapy does not necessarily mean that one's problems are biological, since the failure may stem from the patient's inability or unwillingness to change entrenched ways, or possibly from a mismatch between patient and type of psychological treatment (or a mismatch between patient and therapist).

The psychiatrist can discuss the pros and cons with the patient, whose wishes should be the last word. If a doctor believes the patient's choice is unwise, then the patient should consider another evaluation. Second opinions can be very helpful for patients who feel that the doctor's recommendations are difficult to accept.

Many physicians prefer to combine psychotherapy and medication. They believe the medication will relieve the symptoms, while the psychotherapy will enhance effective social functioning. In many instances medicine makes people accessible to psychotherapy. With the restoration of energy and a zest for life, biologically depressed patients are far better equipped to deal with their internal or life problems effectively.

To us, it seems reasonable to start with medication since it is faster and cheaper and avoids the frustration a biologically depressed person experiences in psychotherapy. Such patients can be demoralized because they are told if they "work" in therapy they will get better. Since they don't get better with psychotherapy—their depression persists—they may even conclude that they are not "good patients" and become more depressed.

We conclude that psychotherapy should not usually be used as a primary (the first) treatment of depressive illness. Unfortunately, many patients with depressive illness are often mistakenly diagnosed, both by psychiatrists and nonpsychiatrists, as having a depression caused by psychological problems and are treated with psychotherapy alone. When the depression fails to respond, many of these therapists then refer the patients to biological psychiatrists for "adjunctive" medication or "medical support."

We think a more reasonable treatment sequence would be to start with medication. Inappropriate psychotherapy not only can delay the relief from painful symptoms (with consequent bad effects on the patient's personal, vocational, and social life) but also can make the patient feel even more helpless when the therapy fails to produce the anticipated improvement. Because psychotherapy usually provides a plausible explanation for the depression, the continuation of the symptoms leaves the patient with a sense of inadequacy and hopelessness.

While the patient is receiving medication, it is useful for him to spend time talking with his psychiatrist. This enables the physician to learn more about the patient and his current life situation. Such knowledge helps the doctor to learn what the specifics of the patient's mood disorder are and how his perceptions and functioning are being affected by his illness. He can then point out to the patient how the depression is affecting other aspects of his behavior. It is one thing to read this book and learn that many depressives have low self-esteem or are pessimistic. It is much more meaningful when a psychiatrist explains to a particular patient how he is devaluing or causing problems for himself because of excessive caution or anger or withdrawal. Such guidance and support can enable the patient to function more effectively and rationally until medication has had an opportunity to work. Continuing visits are important because they support the patient in continuing to take medication. As a first treatment, psychotherapy is probably most appropriate for nonimpaired, nonsuicidal, nonchronic depression without the experiences of loss of pleasure and motivation. Cognitive behavior therapy (CBT) has been extensively recommended. One component of this approach that seems to have therapeutic effect is its strategy of activating and energizing the patient. The cognitive techniques, which aim to change a patient's dysfunctional ideas and dysfunctional social strategies, may offer little additional help to those who are suffering from chronic, disabling depression. There is little evidence that CBT is more effective than placebo.

When psychotherapists refer patients for what they term "supportive" medication, a further problem sometimes arises because of conflict over which of the therapists should be in charge of treatment. We believe that the administrator of medication should have precedence because of the necessity of explaining to the patient the likely origin of his illness. The patient who has been receiving psychotherapy usually has to go through a process of "unlearning" about the causes of his depression. The psychotherapist may have been emphasizing factors that are less relevant or even inaccurate. For example, the psychotherapist may have been focusing on a lengthy exploration of the patient's childhood, which in most instances— contrary to popular notions—has nothing to do with most severe depressions. Conceivably, for some patients psychotherapy may benefit their abnormal physiology, but this is still speculation.

Some patients may refuse medication for emotional illness because they see it as a kind of "crutch" that only a weakling needs. They believe that they should be able to conquer their problems by will power, taking a deep breath, and keeping a stiff upper lip. We think that this occurs because the patients do not understand the causes of mood disorders. (Which is why we are writing this book!) Rather than embarking on the relatively long process of psychotherapy, the patient should instead consult a psychiatrist to determine whether medical interventions would make better sense. When maximally effective, such treatment consists of thorough consultations for several weeks, followed by less frequent, brief followup visits.

Mild Depressions

Most mild depression is "self-limiting"; that is, it goes away by itself, without treatment, so that using medication for mild depression is not always wise. However, chronic, mild depression—dysthymia—may respond to medication. Therefore, mild depression should be monitored professionally to be sure that it does not get worse or become chronic.

Drug Treatment

Many patients have had experience with tranquilizers (such as Valium or Ativan), sedatives (such as Ambien, Dalmane, etc.), or pep pills (such as the amphetamines), but not with antidepressant medications. The medications used in the treatment of the biological depressions have characteristics very different from these more common psychoactive drugs. We describe the antidepressant medications in greater detail in our chapter on drugs, but here we want to make some general comments on the antidepressants as a group.

1. Antidepressant drugs have little effect on normal mood. When taken by normal persons, they may produce slight mental slowing; they do not produce a "high."

2. Antidepressant drugs are "normalizing" in contrast to other drugs affecting mood. For example, amphetamines, which are stimulants, produce a feeling of increased wakefulness, energy, and intellectual activity. If taken by tired, sleepy people, amphetamines temporarily produce a state of normal arousal, and if given to people who are normally aware and alert, they can make them overstimulated ("hyper"). In other words, amphetamines energize regardless of where the individual starts.

At the other extreme, sedatives decrease tension whatever the starting point: if given to overly excited persons, they tend to calm them down; while if given to people who are neither tired nor excited, they may put them to sleep.

In describing the major antidepressant drugs as "normalizing," we mean that they often make a depressed person lose his depressed feelings, but they do not have an effect on the normal person. In this respect they are similar to aspirin. Aspirin lowers a fever but of course does not lower a normal body temperature.

3. The major antidepressant drugs—both the older and new antidepressants as well as lithium and the anticonvulsant drugs—have not been abused because they do not produce high, elated feelings in normal people, although the antidepressants can trigger mania in depressed patients. As we have said earlier, the older major medications have been available for more than 35 years and have never been "sold on the street."

4. Most patients with depression can stop taking the medication and remain nondepressed. Patients who do need to continue taking antidepressants do so because their disease continues, not because they have become dependent on antidepressant medication. A depressed patient who continues to need medication is dependent on it only in the same way that a person with high blood pressure is dependent on medication: he must control the symptoms of a continuing underlying illness.

5. When antidepressants are effective, patients usually continue to derive benefit from them and do not become tolerant to their effects. This also differs from the situation with abusable drugs.

6. Unlike minor tranquilizers and stimulants, which produce benefits within an hour, antidepressants and lithium do not work immediately. The major effects of antidepressants rarely begin before two to four weeks. Insomnia may subside in a week and appetite may come back in two weeks, but such symptoms as lack of interest and motivation take longer to respond. Maximum benefits may take two to three months to develop.

   During treatment, the dosage required may occasionally fluctuate. If some symptoms recur—such as early morning awakening—that is a sign that the dose should be increased before other symptoms reappear.

   Many patients grow discouraged and think a drug has failed because they do not realize it has not been used long enough to work.

7. Side effects often begin when medication is started, before the positive effects begin. The side effects usually decrease with time, but early in treatment the patient may feel that medication is only making him feel worse.

8. The symptoms of depression may be similar from one person to another, but the presumed chemical abnormalities that underlie the symptoms may differ. Unfortunately, no laboratory or chemical tests can as yet predict which drug will be best for a particular individual. A physician may have to try several different drugs before she finds the one that is most effective. Understandably, patients become concerned when this occurs, but it is a situation familiar in other branches of medicine. A good example is high blood pressure. In most instances its chemical causes—like those of depression—are not well understood. Different patients with elevated blood pressure may respond very differently to the same drugs. As with depression, the treating physician often must try several drugs before he obtains the most effective one.

Sometimes a drug is effective but the patient finds the side effects annoying. The newer antidepressants can produce insomnia, somnolence, weight gain, and impaired sexual functioning, but these side effects have wide variation, with some patients experiencing them strongly and some not at all. The most common side effects of the tricyclic antidepressants are dry mouth, constipation, lightheadedness when standing, increased appetite, and weight gain. They may also affect sexual functioning, but in fewer patients than the SSRIs. Monoamine oxidase inhibitors potentially have a more serious side effect that requires special caution. The physician and patient may want to try different medications in the hope of getting equal benefits with fewer side effects.

9. At times, various drugs must be combined. This procedure is also similar to the treatment of hypertension, which may require several medications. The use of more than one medicine at a time requires greater clinical skill.

10. The most effective dose—the best dose for each individual—varies considerably. In extreme instances, some patients may require 30 times the dose required by other patients of a particular medication. Some patients fail to respond because they have been given only a standard dose, since the treating physician does not realize how much dosage requirements differ. Many patients who have received too little medication for their particular needs incorrectly conclude that the drug is of no use to them.

One of the major problems with treatment by family physicians and internists is that, even if they have diagnosed properly and given the right drug, some tend to be cautious and administer too low a dose. Others will employ an adequate dose, but not continue the medication for a long enough period for it to become effective. Therefore, patients often tell psychiatrists that they have been treated with antidepressants that have failed, whereas actually the medications have not been given a fair trial. Although the most common difficulty is too low a dose, another treatment problem is that the medications are not given for a long enough period. Antidepressants cannot be evaluated in less than six weeks.

11. An important feature of psychiatric drugs is that like all other drugs, they may "interact" with other medications. Other drugs may increase or decrease the amount of antidepressant that stays in the body. This can result in either too high or too low levels in the brain. Therefore, it is essential that you keep your psychiatrist informed of all the medications you are taking that may be prescribed by other physicians. Ideally, the physicians should consult with each other prior to any medication changes.

12. Antidepressant medications do not affect the natural history—the lifespan—of the depressive illness. They control the symptoms while nature is taking its healing course. In this respect they are similar to aspirin, which, for example, controls the fever of flu but does not shorten the illness. If aspirin is stopped too soon, the fever will return. If antidepressants are stopped too soon, the patient may relapse. In order to prevent this, most psychiatrists wait six months after a depression has responded before they gradually reduce the dose. If depressive illness is still present, symptoms recur, but an increase in dosage will bring them under control rapidly. If symptoms do not reappear when the drug dosage is reduced, the episode of depression has probably run its course and the medication can be discontinued. Antidepressant medications do not produce severe withdrawal problems on discontinuation. It is always advisable to discontinue any drug slowly. However, if these drugs are discontinued too abruptly, the worst that happens is that patients temporarily have flu-like symptoms.

Patients who have had an abrupt onset to their illness often need only about six months of medication and then can discontinue without immediate relapse, although they may have another depressive episode in the future. Unfortunately, as we mentioned before, 20 to 25 percent of patients will continue to have a mild chronic depression and may require medication for longer periods. It is likely that maintenance medication given to prevent relapse should be given at the same dose level as required for initial symptomatic relief. Antidepressants have been studied carefully for about 30 years in the treatment of large numbers of patients. Since negative side effects from long-term treatment have never been described, we feel relatively comfortable in the long-term administration of the cyclic antidepressants, monoamine oxidase inhibitors, and lithium in patients whose illness is chronic. Our experience with the newer antidepressants is positive, but we are only now developing experience with their long-term use. We think that, in long-term use, they are as safe as the first-generation antidepressants, but we do not have the same 40 years of experience with the new group of drugs. One respect in which the SSRIs are clearly safer is that an overdose of tricyclics can be lethal whereas an SSRI overdose is rarely lethal.

13. Even though the medication may have to be taken for a long time, and the illness may return if the medication is discontinued, one should not conclude that the medication is not very helpful. Most chronic diseases, such as heart disease, diabetes, and arthritis, require continued use of medication for the preservation of good health. The availability of long-term medication for the chronic depressive is a step forward in the treatment of another debilitating illness.

14. One drug—lithium—requires special mention. Lithium is the soluble form—the salt—of a metal and is very similar to sodium, its close chemical relative. Lithium's special use is in the treatment of manic-depressive illness. It can in many cases reduce or eliminate the symptoms of mania and of associated attacks of depression. When lithium is given, the dose must be carefully regulated so that its concentration in the blood is kept within certain limits. Adequate intake of ordinary table salt is also necessary while taking lithium. When the dose is adequately regulated, the patient often experiences no or few side effects. A very few patients develop kidney problems over many years of treatment. Laboratory tests can determine if this is occurring. In these few instances, patients can be treated with other mood stabilizing medications. Lithium is frequently given

on a long-term basis—that is, for many years at a time—as a preventive drug. Its continuous use can reduce the number of episodes of recurrent manic or depressive illness that the manic-depressive patient suffers.

Electroconvulsive Therapy (ECT)

One of the most effective treatments for depressive illness is electroconvulsive therapy (ECT). Seriously depressed patients who do not respond to antidepressant medications have a serious risk of committing suicide. Most of the severely ill patients who fail to respond to medication do respond to ECT. Recently, however, there has been considerable concern about the use of ECT because of the side effects it produced in the past, such as broken bones and memory loss. The idea has also been voiced that ECT is a punishment used to control unpopular behavior. To a great extent, those ideas result from earlier misuse of ECT (analogous to the misuse of digitalis for supposed "heart failure"; digitalis is a life-saving but dangerous drug) and lack of awareness of improvements in the technique.

The failure to recognize that ECT is a medical measure that can reverse serious, often life-threatening illness goes hand in hand with the belief that peculiar behavior is really a sane response to an insane political and social system. According to this belief, there is no such disease as mental illness; all treatment of mental illness is only some form of psychological or behavioral control, and ECT is a particularly punishing form of such control (the book and film *One Flew Over the Cuckoo's Nest* presented this point of view). As we are emphasizing, however, the evidence is now overwhelming that there are indeed biological diseases that produce the disturbed behavior known as mental illness, and these diseases often require medical interventions. No one knows exactly how ECT works, just as no one knows exactly how digitalis works in heart disease or Dilantin in epilepsy, but for suicidal depressive patients who have not responded to medication, ECT is an essential and often life-saving treatment. However, it is our impression that severe "atypical" depressives warrant a trial of MAOIs before considering ECT.

Most of the serious side effects associated with ECT in the past have been eliminated by modern techniques. When electroconvulsive treatment was first introduced, patients received neither anesthesia nor muscle relaxants and were conscious until the seizure rendered them unconscious. Lying on the bed awaiting the shock was very anxiety provoking, and patients became increasingly upset with successive treatments. In some instances the force of the convulsion was very strong, and the muscle contractions produced broken bones. Following the treatment, some patients reported substantial memory loss.

The modern procedure, which has largely eliminated these concerns, involves the administration of a general anesthetic and a short-acting muscle relaxant. The patient is asleep when the therapeutic electrical impulse is delivered to the brain, he feels nothing, and his body does not convulse. Approximately two minutes after the administration of the anesthetic, the patient awakens. He is generally slightly confused, because of both a barbiturate hangover and the treatment itself. He is likely to remain tired and to feel somewhat fuzzy for the remainder of the day. When he has been treated as an outpatient, which is a frequent practice, someone must drive the patient home.

ECT is usually given three times per week. More frequent administrations do not seem to increase the rate of recovery. The total number of treatments required varies considerably but usually is between six and twelve—that is, the total duration of treatment is two to four weeks. Following the completion of the course of therapy, many patients do have some memory deficits for the period before ECT was begun, particularly for the period of their illness. These memory deficits tend to disappear with time, and in most instances patients suffer little chronic memory loss. Measuring the extent of the memory loss is complicated because depression itself impairs concentration and memory; the memory deficits of which the patient complains may be the product of the preexisting depression rather than of the ECT. Recent changes in the placement of electrodes—on one side of the head (unilateral) rather than both sides (bilateral)—have also decreased the amount of memory loss and temporary confusion.

The major problems still remaining in the administration of ECT arise from the use of general anesthetic (which always involves some risk) and from the small possibility of permanent noticeable memory loss. In a person who is physically healthy except for the severe depression, the risk of a fatal reaction to the anesthesia is minimal. The risk of memory loss affects people in different ways. A legal scholar, for example, might be handicapped by such a loss, but for many people it would be only a minor nuisance.

In judging whether ECT is advisable for a particular patient, one must above all *weigh the risks of anesthesia and some memory loss against the threat of suicide (again, individuals with severe depression have a 10 to 30 percent suicide mortality rate).* The presence of severe impairments, such as inability to eat and prolonged social and vocational withdrawal, can also affect the decision. On the whole we believe ECT is underused in depressed patients who have not benefited from medication. (ECT, however, is of no value in panic disorder or other anxiety states.)

In some instances of severe depression and mania where electroconvulsive therapy is the treatment of choice, the patient will refuse to accept such treatment and a decision must be made by the physician and the family about administering ECT involuntarily. These crises arise infrequently, but in severe illness the family must be prepared for such a decision.

Psychological Management of Depression

Although we believe that for major biological depression, medication is the immediate treatment of choice, psychotherapy is of value in several circumstances. In mild depressions, particularly those that seem related to life stresses, psychotherapy is often a useful initial treatment (if a complete psychiatric diagnosis has ruled out biological depression). It is also helpful as a supplementary treatment directed at the psychological consequences of severe depression.

Occasionally, psychotherapy has distinct value in helping to resolve a chronically unrewarding life situation that worsens depression. In particular, marital counseling may have a role since unsatisfactory marriages seem extremely common in the environment of depressed patients. It's often not quite clear whether the unsatisfactory marriage leads to the depression, or vice versa, but anything that makes an unsatisfactory marriage better can only be useful. Also, at times, marital counseling helps to allow a civilized breakup of a crumbling marriage, with benefit to both parties.

Psychotherapy for Depressive Reactions to Life Stress

As we have pointed out, mild depressions can be biological in origin, but sometimes they are normal human reactions of sadness and grief to unavoidable experiences of loss or disappointment. In distinguishing depressive illness from ordinary sadness, the psychiatrist watches for such symptoms of depressive illness as loss of pleasure, appetite and sleep changes, energy loss, low self-esteem, and guilt.

The diagnosis is not made strictly in terms of the depth of the depression, because depressive illness can be either severe or mild, and the same is true of sadness and unhappiness resulting from unsatisfactory or tragic relationships with family, friends, and employers. Mild depressive *illness* responds best to medication, while even prolonged depression resulting from life's misfortunes may do poorly on antidepressant medications. Such unhappiness may respond to time, to change, and, in some instances, to psychotherapy.

Psychological Therapy for the Patient Successfully Treated with Medication

The fact that medication is of clearly documented, specific effectiveness in depressive illness does not imply that additional psychological treatment is of no value. Even when responsive to medication, the depressive patient may have lingering symptoms that are complications of the illness itself; sometimes personal limitations and life stresses contribute to these persistent symptoms. In many instances patients will benefit by a combination of medication, psychological therapy, training in new social habits, and possibly even a change of lifestyle.

A frequent psychological consequence of depressive illness, particularly if the depression has lasted for a long time, is demoralization. *Demoralization* refers to feelings of ineffectuality, inadequacy at solving problems, and inability to control one's life; it can result from biologically produced depression as well as from external events. The depressed person lacks drive, motivation, and the ability to face the challenges posed by complex personal problems—and all this can result from the biological illness. Countless marital and other personal problems often develop as a result of depressive and manic-depressive illness. Serious marital problems probably occur in at least half of the couples in which one member is manic-depressive. In such situations, couple therapy or family therapy focusing on such problems may be of benefit.

Psychological problems produced by the illness frequently outlive the illness itself. They are not neurotic problems. They are not the result of the person's incorrect perception of the world and himself. They are the realistic consequences of his former inabilities. A medical analogy might be a treated broken leg. After the bone is healed and the cast is removed, the patient may have to exercise his leg before he can work normally again. Although the bone is no longer fractured, the muscles have weakened and must be exercised to regain their former strength. Just as weakened muscles are a physiological complication of such an injury, demoralization can be the psychological complication of depression.

The demoralization produced by depression often disappears with time, especially in the presence of fortunate and pleasurable life experiences. However, psychological therapy may accelerate the process. A variety of other psychologically potent forces can also help, such as patient support groups, religious groups, social organizations, consciousness-raising groups, and encounter groups.

The Relationship of the Doctor and the Patient

In any medical treatment the patient must feel comfortable with her doctor, and this is especially important in the treatment of biological depression. The doctor and patient must develop sufficient rapport so that the patient feels free to discuss all of her medical and psychological concerns. Otherwise such factors as side effects or unexpected complications in the patient's personal life might keep her from following the instructions for taking the antidepressant drugs and thus seriously limit their effectiveness. Whether the treating physician is a general practitioner, psychiatrist, or psychopharmacologist, if the patient is dissatisfied with the relationship, she should see another doctor.

The Family's Role in the Treatment of Depression and Manic-Depression

Biological psychiatrists differ little in the degree to which they want the family to be involved when the patient is seriously ill. They want to explain to the family what the nature of the problem is, the kind of treatment that is being administered, when treatment response should be expected, and the alternative plans that are available if the current treatment program is not working well. Specific information applicable to depression and to mania is particularly important to family members. We summarize this information in the following pages.

Depression

In counseling families on how to help a depressive patient, we try to make several points. First and uppermost, *the patient has an illness.*

Second, the patient is not trying to exploit the family members. Depressed patients have feelings of hopelessness, decreased initiative, and feelings of helplessness. They need help to perform many activities they could easily handle alone when well; when the depression becomes more severe, they are unable to perform such activities even with help.

Third, as our case examples illustrate, the patient's illness can disrupt and disorganize family life. At the simplest level, for adults, there is often a loss of function. The wage earner may work less effectively and sometimes cannot work at all. The housewife neglects her house or children. Depressed patients can also be extremely difficult to live with. In contrast to a family member who is psychotic and hears voices or has visions, depressives have problems that appear to be only exaggerations of normal human problems. It is easy for family members to understand that a psychotic person is ill, but depressed individuals may not seem to have a disease. They often engender familial unhappiness and anger by being a "wet blanket." They do not enjoy things. They do not initiate activities—they must be pushed or pulled. They do not fulfill appropriate duties in their relationships. It is difficult not to see this as laziness or selfishness if the family does not recognize the real pain involved. The black, pessimistic views of these patients become tedious. Things are not good, things never were any good, things will never be any good. They may be irritable, complaining, a "sour puss." They are not affectionate—in depression, many lose feelings of warmth and love. Since depressives are uninterested in sex, it is difficult for their partners not to experience this as rejection and as lack of love. Other members of the family tend to react with resentment and anger and to distance themselves from the sufferer. Because depressed patients have feelings of helplessness and feel increasingly dependent, such reactions, even though completely understandable, may worsen the depression.

Fourth, in some instances the depressive's feelings may be completely unrelated to what is really happening in her life. The depressive's business, marriage, and children may be flourishing, and yet she will feel that life is empty and barren. It is pointless to say, "Look at all you have to live for." Her feelings are irrational, and she cannot be argued out of them. When she says, "I'm no good…. My life has been a failure….Things will not get better," telling her that she's mistaken is not useful and may add to her demoralization. Notice that we are not saying that the family members should agree with the patient, but merely that they should not try to talk her out of her feelings, since she experiences such arguments as another putdown. It *is* useful for family members to tell the patient that they are sorry that she feels so bad and to remind her that these feelings are a part of the depressive illness and will eventually diminish. The family's job is to maintain optimism and perspective.

The most serious symptom the family must recognize in a depressed person is suicidal thinking. When a depressive illness has become that severe, skilled professional help is necessary immediately. The depressed person often—*but not always*—expresses the suicidal feelings he experiences, saying, for example, "Life is not worth living," or "I'd be better off dead," or "Life seems purposeless." Furthermore, because the mood of some suicidal patients lifts when they finally decide to commit suicide, the family should not take an apparent improvement at face value. *When family members are in doubt, they should seek a psychiatric consultation at once.* When they are in doubt, they cannot leave matters to the patient. Depressed patients who are suicidal may, because of their feelings of grave pessimism, reject any notion that treatment could be of help. In some instances the depressed patient must be hospitalized involuntarily. If the family suspects that the situation calls for hospitalization and the patient does not have a psychiatrist, they should contact the psychiatric crisis unit at a large hospital. If none are available, they should call the police. In many localities the police have been trained to deal with psychiatric emergencies and can help take the depressed patient to an appropriate treatment unit.

Occasionally, a depressed patient may not want the family involved. If so, he and the doctor should discuss that option and come to a decision together.

Mania

Sometimes the family recognizes manic illness long before the patient does. He or she is oblivious to the change from normal good mood to the euphoria or irritability that increases as the illness worsens. If the patient has been treated before and especially if he is under continuing treatment with a therapist, he is more likely to listen to the family and get emergency help from his psychiatrist or from a crisis unit. If the patient is unwilling to comply, the family should obtain expert opinion about the advisability of involuntary hospitalization. The manic's behavior may be dangerous not only to himself but to his family as well because of his impaired judgment. Formerly conservative individuals may go out on wild spending sprees, speculate with the family's savings, impulsively engage in unwise business decisions, initiate one or several sexual liaisons, and so forth. This behavior can result in permanent damage to the family's finances and destroy the relationship with the spouse or significant other.

In extreme cases manic patients may minimize or completely deny the presence of illness and refuse treatment. In such instances involuntary hospitalization is a *must*, and the family should obtain help, either from the patient's psychiatrist, a family physician, the local crisis center, or the hospital emergency ward. Involuntary hospitalization of the manic patient may be very difficult for the family because of the patient's anger and defiance. Nevertheless, for both the patient's and the family's welfare, treatment is absolutely essential, and the family must persist in obtaining it regardless of the patient's objections.

Self- and Family Monitoring of Depression

A patient with depressive illness or mania should learn to evaluate and measure her own mood. The patient usually sees a physician once a week when a medication has first been prescribed and is still being adjusted, but after that, visits become less frequent. Therefore, the patient should learn how to determine if she is getting better or worse, in both her feelings and her behavior.

Toward this end each patient should learn her own "target symptoms." Each individual patient does not necessarily have all the symptoms seen in depression and mania. Accordingly, two people may both have profound biological depressions and yet have only some symptoms in common.

For example, both may have no zest for life—they may have lost interest in their usual activities and they may often feel sad and even suicidal. However, one may feel guilty while the other does not; one may sleep 20 hours a day and the other only four; one may eat compulsively and gain weight, whereas the other has a marked loss of appetite and loses considerable weight. One may be agitated and constantly in motion, while the other moves slowly as if struck in molasses. The first patient may skip from subject to subject, whereas the other's mind may move so slowly that she forgets her first sentence by the time she has completed her second. The same variation occurs in mania. One manic may seem fine and act as if ecstatically happy, while another may be extremely irritable and angry.

In order to evaluate himself properly and to help the physician to evaluate his progress, the patient should learn the particular symptoms he gets when he becomes depressed or manic. Armed with this knowledge, both the patient and the physician can tell when the depression or mania is improving or when—say, in a period when the patient has stopped taking medicine—the first mild but important warning symptoms appear.

Many psychiatrists will ask a depressed patient how she feels on a one-to-ten scale—with one as the worst ever and ten the best. While depressed the patient is likely to assign herself an unrealistically high number—for example, she might report that she is much closer to normal than she really is, giving her mood a "six." When medication and therapy have restored her mood to normal, she sees that her previous reports have been inaccurate—that her mood was really a "three." This is because each time the patient is in the middle of a depressed episode she cannot remember exactly what it was like to feel good. When she receives effective treatment and returns to her normal mood, she is surprised how good it is to feel normal.

If one notices improvement, it is helpful to report to the physician that one feels better this week compared to last week, but one can feel better and still not be functioning very well. The real question is how the patient is doing in objective, descriptive terms. How much time is she spending in activities that she usually enjoys—gardening, playing tennis and bridge, refinishing furniture? How much time is he spending fishing, playing chess, finishing the basement, or participating in the men's softball league? This is the best way of assessing change for the better or worse, since depressives forget not only how good they should *feel* but what they *do* when normal.

Although the symptoms of depression and mania are to a great extent inside the patient's head, effects of the illness are clear-cut enough to be visible to an outsider. This means that other people can be helpful in determining the patient's progress or lack of progress. For example, a depressed patient may report that his interest in life is returning and that therefore he is well on his way to normality, but his spouse can tell the examining physician how the patient's interests are still different from his previous ones.

Similarly, because the depressed patient is often quite unaware of her behavior and how it appears to others, her family may be in a better position to report signs that the treatment may not be going well—for example, unusual tensions, irritability, withdrawal, and lack of affection. As we mentioned earlier, this is particularly important if the patient is manic. The manic's self-observation is often much less accurate than that of the depressive, for the illness itself makes him feel good, think well of himself, be optimistic about his future accomplishments, and think continuing treatment a waste of time. In addition, one special caution is necessary with the manic-depressive: when such patients have been depressed and then begin to recover, they may "overshoot" and become mildly manic—they exhibit *hypomania*. Everyone around them may be so pleased with the disappearance of the depressive symptoms that they fail to perceive that the patient now has the opposite face of the illness. It is important to recognize hypomania as a symptom of illness because of the severe difficulties that may follow.

Self-monitoring and family monitoring are important because even after a patient has responded well to treatment, his or her need for medication often fluctuates. On a constant dose, one patient may experience bouts of depression, while another may experience periods of pleasant but potentially destructive highs. This reflects the fact that their disease causes unusual medical responses. (As we said earlier, individuals not suffering from depression would experience no such "highs.") The treated person with a mood disorder is somewhat like a diabetic. The diabetic's body cannot chemically process the carbo-hydrate and sugar in his diet, and he must administer the hor-mone insulin to himself in order to normalize his metabolism. However, the diabetic's best dose of insulin depends not only on the nature of his faulty metabolism but also on the type and amount of food he eats, his physical activity, and the presence of other illnesses. All these factors may require him to increase or decrease his daily insulin dose. The doctor must teach the patient to measure the effects of these experiences on his dia-betes and how to adjust his diet and medication himself.

Most biological psychiatrists do not assign such responsi-bilities to the depressed patient, either because the adjustments are more complex or because psychiatrists have been more con-servative in this regard. However, the patient must realize that his or her need for medication may vary, depending on stress, illness, and personal experiences. On a fixed and apparently adequate dose of medication, her psychological motor may not run smoothly. It may sputter and miss even when it is warmed up. The patient must learn to observe these misfirings and com-municate them quickly to the physician, who will help the pa-tient to adjust her medication. This will minimize fluctuations in the effectiveness of treatment. Like many other medical treat-ments, treatment for depression can be very good but does re-quire constant supervision and adjustment.

6

A Brief Guide to
Psychopharmacological
Drugs

THIS CHAPTER will provide an overview of the types
of drugs used in the treatment of depression, manic-depression,
and illnesses related to depression (panic disorder and atypical
depression; see next chapter). However, the dosage of the drugs,
whether they should be increased over time, whether they
should be taken on an empty stomach or between meals, the
time of day they should be taken, and the particular side effects
of each should all be discussed in detail with the treating physician. There are a number of acceptable ways of administering
each medication.

Before describing the major classes of drugs, we wish to make
a few comments about drugs in general.

1. *Names of drug classes.* The names of drug classes are frequently based on one of their therapeutic effects, but they
   may be used in the treatment of other disorders as well. For
   example, the drugs used in the treatment of depression—

antidepressants—may be used to treat bedwetting in children, panic attacks in adults, and excessive shyness in some people (social phobia).

2. *Side effects.* Side effects are unwanted, fairly common, predictable effects produced by drugs. Although side effects have varying degrees of unpleasantness, they are rarely life-threatening. Not all drugs have appreciable side effects, and many produce side effects only in some of the people who take them. For example, someone who is not allergic to penicillin (see point 3) will feel no different taking a therapeutic dose of that drug than if he had taken nothing at all. Even very large doses of penicillin produce no side effects in such people. With aspirin, however, the situation is different. The doses necessary to relieve headache rarely produce uncomfortable symptoms, but when larger doses of aspirin are used—such as those that are sometimes necessary to control the pain and inflammation of arthritis—many people develop side effects such as gastric irritation, abdominal discomfort, or ringing in their ears. The gastric irritation produced by aspirin can produce an ulcer, which in some instances can be dangerous, but this is very rare.

Drugs differ not only in the proportion of people in whom they produce side effects, but in their range of side effects. For instance, tricyclic antidepressants cause most people to develop dry mouth and constipation. We will discuss the more common side effects and the specific hazards, if any, of the psychopharmacological drugs. Some drugs that carry side-effect risks are the best treatments for particular illnesses. In such instances, the physician who recommends them will carefully monitor the patient at regular intervals to determine whether drug toxicity is developing and whether the drug should be stopped. In our discussion we will identify these drugs and describe the test procedures.

Even though the Food and Drug Administration (FDA) will release a drug to the market only when convinced of its safety and effectiveness, the rare side effect—that is, one that occurs in less than 1 in a 1,000 cases—cannot possibly be picked up prior to market release because of the limited number of subjects studied. In order to detect rare side effects, our society will have to invest the resources necessary to track both the drug use and the drug reactions that occur after a drug has been released for marketing by following each patient who receives the drug. The entire area is extremely controversial. The hope of zero risk can never be achieved. Any drug that helps may on occasion injure. Poisonous drugs should be removed from the market, but useful ones should not, and some, like anticancer drugs, are both poisonous and helpful. The problem is that our current system allows us to tell one from the other before market release with regard to common side effects, but is not effective for detecting rare, and possibly severe, side effects. Postmarketing surveillance is discussed in more detail in the final chapter.

The purpose of this book is to help the potential patient to go about receiving informed professional care. Once the patient is receiving such care, it is quite understandable that he or she might wish to know more detail about potential side effects of the medication she is receiving. To discuss these in detail would obscure the purpose of our book. *Handbook of Psychiatric Drugs, 2004 Edition*, by J. Albers, M.D., Rhoda K. Hahn, M.D., and Christopher Reist, M.D. (Current Clinical Strategies Publishing, www.ccspublishing.com/ccs, 27071 Cabot Road, Laguna Hills, CA 92653-7011) provides a detailed, rational discussion of the variety of side effects that might result from psychotropic drug treatment. Most of these side effects are trivial and easily managed. If more information is needed about any particular medication, we heartily recommend that the reader obtain a copy of Dr. Albers' book. A valuable and authoritative Web site dealing with psychiatric drugs is http.//www.dr-bob.org/.

3. *Idiosyncratic reactions to drugs.*   Idiosyncratic reactions, which arise infrequently, can produce life-threatening medical problems. For example, after repeated treatment with penicillin, some people develop an allergy to it. Their sensitivity to it is so great that they may develop an allergic

reaction when an injection of a different substance is administered from a syringe previously used for penicillin, even though the syringe has been thoroughly washed and heated to temperatures above that of boiling water (that is one of the reasons for using disposable syringes). In rare instances penicillin allergy produces swelling of the larynx, which may in turn cause choking and even death. Some drugs are more likely than others to produce these idiosyncratic toxic effects.

4. *The comparative effectiveness of the antidepressants.*   An obvious question is how effective are the different antidepressants compared to one another? Another obvious question is which of the conditions discussed respond better to a particular antidepressant than others? The surprising answer to the first question is that there are very few studies comparing two antidepressants. Most drug studies are funded by the pharmaceutical industry. They usually do not want to conduct comparison studies for fear that their drug will prove less effective than others. They may conduct comparative trials if they are trying to break into the market after their drug has been approved by the Food and Drug Administration. Such studies are up to the drug manufacturer and can be subtly biased in terms of the dosage they administer of the comparative drug (for example, using too high or too low a dose). As a result, we do not know the most effective drugs, nor do we know which is the best drug to employ if a patient fails to respond to the first drug tried. With regard to the second question, there are some depressive disorders known to respond better to one type of antidepressant than another. An example is adolescent-onset or chronic atypical depression, which responds to treatment with the MAOIs, but does not respond to the tricyclic antidepressants.

Since we, in general, do not know which patient will do best on which drug, we tell depressed patients that there are several good treatments, that some patients clearly do better on one drug than another, but there are no tests predicting the best response in advance of taking a drug. We may have to try several drugs, and we warn our patients that they will have to be patient. Jumping quickly from one drug to another is a self-defeating practice.

5. *Combining medications.*   Because drugs interact with each other, if a patient takes several drugs simultaneously the chances for developing side effects are greatly increased. Therefore, it pays to keep the treatment as simple as possible. The majority of depressed patients can be satisfactorily treated with a single antidepressant and no other medication. If patients require multiple medications, this usually is discovered only after a single medication has proven ineffective. Some psychopharmacologists commonly initiate treatment with three or more different medications at the same time. We think this is a serious error and that it would be wise to get another opinion under these circumstances. If effective treatment for a particular patient requires the use of several medications at the same time, such a pattern usually becomes apparent only after successive steps.

6. *Generic drugs.*   In marketing a new drug, a drug company assigns it both a *generic* name related to its chemical components and a *trade* name (brand name). For example, Ciba-Geigy markets the drug imipramine (generic name) under the trade name Tofranil. Lilly marketed the drug fluoxetine (generic name) under the trade name Prozac. Drug companies patent new drugs that they develop and retain the sole right to manufacture them until the patent expires. At that time, any pharmaceutical company may manufacture the drug, often giving it a new brand name.

A new drug can be marketed only after passing numerous tests reviewed by the FDA, which certifies the drug's safety and effectiveness. The FDA's overseeing of imitative generic drugs produced after the expiration of the original patents is less extensive. Effectiveness has already been documented, and the FDA permits marketing of the drug so long as it has been shown to be "equivalently available" to the body—that is, as easily absorbed—as the original drug. There is some question as to whether such monitoring of generic drugs is always sufficient. The FDA also permits some variation in the amount of the trade-name drug contained in the new generic: it can range from 80 to 120 percent.

The issue of generic drugs is important both because their price is often substantially less than that of brand-name drugs and because of the permitted variations in the amount of the active ingredients and any additives. Individuals being switched from a trade-name drug to a generic may experience overdosage or underdosage. There have been many letters to psychiatric journals about patients whose illness recurred when they were switched from the trade-name drug to the new generic; presumably, they were underdosed with the generic. Some patients have become toxic, presumably because they were receiving too much of the generic drug.

If there is consistent quality control, a generic that varies from the trade-name drug is perfectly acceptable—for example, if it always contains 120 percent of the brand-name drug or always contains 80 percent of the brand-name drug. But if the percentage varies from batch to batch, the patient will receive different doses of the active medication at different times, even if the label states that the amount is the same. It should be emphasized that brand-name drugs are also subject to quality-control problems. It is not uncommon for drug companies—like automobile manufacturers—to issue recall notices because of defective manufacture.

With these various cautions in mind, it is obviously in the interest of the consumer to purchase the generic if it is cheaper than the brand-name product and equally effective. But we have one more warning here. Because generic brands may vary among themselves, the patient should be sure that each time his prescription is refilled *he receives the generic drug produced by a particular company.*

A final overall cautionary note. If a patient has been maintained on the same brand-name drug or the same company's generic drug with satisfactory results, and his symptoms recur when his prescription is refilled, there is a possibility that the quality control failed and that he has received a batch of defective pills. The best way to test for this is to have the pharmacist look at the wholesale lot from which the patient's prescription was drawn and to obtain an equivalent medication from a different wholesale lot.

Side Effects and the
Physician's Desk Reference (PDR)

Many of our patients look up drugs they are taking on the web and are sometimes dismayed at the large number of side effects (often severe) that have been associated with a particular drug. These side effects are listed in detail in the *Physician's Desk Reference*, also called the *PDR*, which is really a compilation of the package inserts provided by drug companies for their products. Before refusing to take such a drug, it is useful for readers to know the functions of the *PDR* and how package inserts are constructed. The important point is that the *PDR* "package insert" is not only to inform a physician (or patient), but to protect the drug company legally. To be marketed, a drug must be found by the FDA to be effective and safe. This is usually determined by the results in about 2,000 people. The drug company then counts side effects on the drug (and placebo) and divides this number by the number who received the drug or placebo. This calculates the percentage risks of side effects. For statistical reasons, one cannot be sure of the presence or absence of uncommon side effects in such small studies.

When the drug is marketed and physicians begin to prescribe it, they may notify the FDA or drug manufacturer that they have treated a patient who developed some unwanted, possibly severe, side effect while on the drug. (But physicians don't have to notify, and most do not.) The difficulty is that we cannot determine the percentage of patients who experience side effects on the drug, because we do not know how many received the drug. After a drug is marketed, no records are made of everyone receiving the drug so that millions of people may have received the medication in question. Therefore we cannot determine the proportion of patients in which a particular side effect occurs. Its rate of occurrence may be very, very small.

The package insert includes all side effects of which the company has been notified. It often also includes side effects that have been reported as occurring in that class of drugs, even if there has been no such report about this particular drug. The drug company then publishes a list of these, so that if any patient anywhere develops what may be a one in a million side effect, the drug company can state that it listed this side effect in the package insert, so they cannot be sued for concealing any of the drug's dangers. Finally, it is possible that the reported side effects have nothing to do with the drug and may have been due to the illness or even another illness. A major public health advance would be the development of a systematic postmarketing surveillance system.

The Second-Generation Antidepressants

Selective Serotonin Reuptake Inhibitors (SSRIs)

These are a familiar group of drugs, of which Prozac was the first marketed. Some drugs in this same category are Celexa, Lexapro, Luvox, Paxil, and Zoloft. All are believed to increase the activity of serotonin, an important neurotransmitter. In general, these drugs have fewer side effects than the tricyclic antidepressants, though individuals taking SSRIs can experience a decrease in sexual interest and difficulty reaching orgasm. Many patients who do not respond to the older antidepressants respond to the SSRIs. But the reverse is also true. Some patients do not respond to SSRIs, but do respond to older antidepressants. Of the new antidepressants, all SSRIs appear equally effective. It is not clear if there is any benefit to switching from one to another, although side effects differ. A problem with all is that the lowest manufactured drug dose may be too great for some patients and it is necessary to either dilute them with apple juice or Gatorade, or cut them up.

Side Effects.   The SSRIs produce drowsiness in some people and agitation and edginess in others. Agitation is described by some as a feeling of "edginess," which may be avoided by taking smaller doses. Some patients, however, simply cannot tolerate the drug at all. There is also serious concern as to whether SSRIs may at times increase depression and suicidal impulses. Some patients have become more depressed—and even suicidal—while taking SSRIs. This has led to lawsuits. It is not known whether such reactions were due to SSRIs or were in spite of SSRIs. Studies that have compared the rate of suicidal ideation and suicidal attempts in patients treated with SSRIs to that in patients treated with other antidepressants have not demonstrated any difference. We believe that if such an effect does occur with SSRIs it is extremely uncommon. It would be unfortunate if fear of such reactions, which have not been substantiated, prevented patients from accepting properly monitored treatment with this useful medication.

Patients with spontaneous panic attacks who are treated with ordinary doses (20 mg) of Prozac do experience marked increases in anxiety about half the time. Nonetheless, such patients usually benefit from SSRIs if started with one-tenth to one-quarter of the standard starting dose. Zoloft also is not well tolerated in the usual starting dose of 50 mg daily. However, most patients with panic disorder do seem to be able to tolerate initial doses of 25 mg daily. Paxil has been reported as tolerable at 10 mg daily as an initial dose. The starting dose for the other SSRIs in patients with panic disorder is not known; presumably, they too would have to start at anywhere from one-tenth to one-quarter of the usual starting dose.

At first, it was thought that Prozac did not produce the weight gain seen with other antidepressants. Apparently, weight loss occurs in some people initially but is followed by a return to normal weight or sometimes by weight gain. Prozac produces the same adverse sexual side effects as other antidepressants in roughly one-third of patients, as with the other drugs. These include decreased sexual desire, decreased erectile potency in men, decreased vaginal lubrication in women, and either delayed or blocked orgasm in men and women. Counteracting medications can often lessen these effects. After taking SSRIs for a period of time, some patients experience what has been referred to as "poop out." Poop out is not a return of the original depressive symptoms. What people report is a subtle loss of interest and incentive in life. These symptoms can often be reversed by the administration of the SSRI with certain other drugs, such as Wellbutrin or a stimulant drug such as Ritalin or amphetamine. Other patients do experience a return of all of their symptoms. In some instances, they may respond to an increased dose of the SSRI, while in others an increased dose does not produce the initial good response.

Prozac and suicidal preoccupation. After Prozac had been on the market for some years, there was a report that a small number of patients became preoccupied with suicide when on Prozac. All of these patients, however, had been chronically ill and had suicidal preoccupations previously.

Obviously, it is very difficult when you are treating depressed people, who are often suicidal, to determine whether a medication you have given them has increased or decreased their suicidal impulses or thoughts. Is it because of the medicine or in spite of it? The only really scientific way to determine this is to assign a group of patients randomly to the drug in question or to a standard drug, and then to have the patients evaluated by psychiatrists who do not know which drug the patient is on. Such studies, as one might imagine, are extremely rare.

It is well known that any drug may occasionally have unpleasant or even intolerable side effects. If the patient is already in substantial difficulty, the addition of new distress may well increase hopelessness and suicidal thoughts in an already depressed patient.

Prozac was marketed in a capsule of 20 mg. In most depressed patients, this dosage is well tolerated. However, experienced biological psychiatrists have found that some people may become agitated on this dose although they can tolerate a lower dose.

Recently, there have been frightening claims that paroxetine (Paxil) and venlafaxine (Effexor) increase suicide attempts in children. These claims are inaccurate. No actual suicide occurred in any of the studies in question. What did occur is that on self-rating forms, approximately 1 percent of placebo-treated patients reported suicidal thoughts, whereas approximately 2 percent of drug-treated patients stated this.

There has been no published evidence that this small increase in reports of "suicidal thoughts" is linked to any worsening of outcome. More important, in the large multisite trials studying these medications in children, these particular drugs were not especially useful in treating depression. So for this reason, Paxil and Effexor should not be used with children and adolescents.

Wellbutrin (bupropion)

Wellbutrin is another recently introduced antidepressant whose mode of functioning is unclear. Its overall effectiveness is said to be similar to that of the traditional agents, but there is no information about its effectiveness compared to the other newer antidepressant agents.

Side effects. A major advantage of bupropion that distinguishes it from other antidepressants is that it does not cause weight gain or impaired sexual functioning. It also does not cause drying of the mouth and constipation. Some patients, however, may become agitated on this medication. It is often a useful adjunctive medicine for SSRIs, lessening fatigue and sexual side effects.

Effexor (venlafaxine)

Effexor is a drug that not only inhibits serotonin reuptake, but in higher doses inhibits reuptake of norepinephrine. Deficiencies of norepinephrine in the brain are *thought* to be a cause of some depressions, and Effexor, because of its "dual" action on serotonin and norepinephrine, might be more effective for some patients. However, this remains speculative. Demonstration would require a comprehensive research evaluation.

Side effects. If Effexor is begun at too high a dose, patients often report that they develop diarrhea or nausea. Therefore, Effexor should be begun at a low dose and gradually increased slowly enough to minimize these side effects. Other side effects include dizziness, sleepiness, and insomnia. When doses of 300 mg or greater per day are reached, blood pressure sometimes increases. For this reason, the physicians will monitor the patient's blood pressure. If a patient's blood pressure is elevated, but the response to Effexor is favorable, a medication to lower blood pressure will be prescribed. As with the SSRIs, weight loss occurs in some people, but is followed by a return to normal weight and sometimes to weight gain. Effexor produces the same adverse sexual side effects as the SSRIs in roughly one-third of patients. Counteracting medications can sometimes lessen these effects.

Serzone (nefazodone)

Serzone is a relatively new antidepressant whose effectiveness, compared to the drugs already mentioned, is not known but is conventionally believed to be effective in a smaller proportion of depressives. Its two major advantages compared to the antidepressants mentioned so far (except Wellbutrin) are that it does not produce weight gain and does not affect sexual functioning. Recently, there have been reports of serious liver failure and deaths in patients receiving Serzone. The risk is very slight and it is possible that it can be reduced by obtaining periodic liver function tests.

Side effects. The most common side effects are dizziness and lowered blood pressure. Some patients may also experience muddling of their thinking and problems with memory.

Remeron (mirtazapine)

Remeron is another fairly recent antidepressant. Its effects on the brain are different from those of any medications discussed so far, but may involve two neurotransmitters we have seen before, serotonin and norepinephrine. It lacks the side effects produced by the SSRIs and Effexor (nausea, insomnia, and sexual dysfunction).

Side effects. The most common side effects are sleepiness, increased appetite, weight gain, and dizziness. It tends to make many patients fat and sedated. A rare side effect may be that it decreases white cells in the blood, which predisposes to infection. Any patient taking Remeron who develops the sudden onset of sore throat, inflammation of the mouth, or high fever should report this to his physician immediately.

The First-Generation Antidepressants

Tricyclic Antidepressants

The tricyclic antidepressants were one of the first two classes of drugs used to treat depressive illnesses. They have been used for 40 years and until recently were the first drugs a psychiatrist would try with a new depressed patient. They are thought to work, as mentioned earlier, by preventing the secreting cells from reabsorbing such neurotransmitters as serotonin and norepinephrine. Some tricyclic antidepressants have a greater effect on norepinephrine and some a greater effect on serotonin. Overall, they are almost equally effective, but some patients will do better on one or tolerate one better than another.

For example, amitriptyline has the greatest sedative effect, and although useful in some agitated patients, may leave others too groggy throughout the day. Other tricyclic antidepressants, such as desipramine or protriptyline, are on occasion "activating." Some patients who have been slowed down mentally and physically may find that these drugs restore their energy and relieve their depression, but other patients may become too agitated by them. These rules are not hard and fast. Some patients are relaxed or sedated by the "activating drugs," while others may be activated by the more "sedative drugs."

Side Effects.   Dry mouth, constipation, blurred vision, lowered blood pressure (with dizziness after standing up quickly, though these medications also can elevate blood pressure), weight gain, and such sexual side effects as decrease of sexual desire in men and women, decreased erectile potency in men, decreased vaginal lubrication in women, and either delayed or blocked orgasm in men and women are among the most common side effects.

Management of the effects.   After the depression has been relieved, the physician will often attempt to lower the dose to see if she can obtain a satisfactory "tradeoff" between symptom relief and side effects. She hopes that the lower dose will decrease undesirable side effects and still keep the depression under control. However, recent studies have indicated that patients may do better during maintenance drug treatment if their medication level is *not* cut from their initial treatment dose. It seems advisable to maintain the dose at as high a level as is necessary, depending on the patient's particular side effects and how he tolerates them. Sometimes the side effects disappear with the passage of time. When they do not, relatively simple techniques to counteract them are often effective. The dry mouth can be counteracted by sugarless "sourballs." Light-headedness on standing up can be prevented by sitting for a moment before standing. Patients troubled with such hypotension may also have to avoid hot baths. Increased fluid intake and bulk laxatives (such as Metamucil) may decrease constipation. Certain drugs (e.g., cyproheptadine, urecholine) can be used to relieve the sexual side effects produced by these agents. To counteract weight gain—which may come from a decreased "basal metabolic rate"—the patient must resort to the customary measures of reduced calorie intake and increased physical activity.

Monoamine Oxidase Inhibitors (MAOIs)

These drugs, introduced at about the same time as the tricyclic antidepressants, were widely used in Europe, and are used infrequently in the United States. The reason for such caution in the United States was the possibility that, if taken in combination with certain foods or other medications, these drugs might produce an episode of dangerously high blood pressure. The monoamine oxidase inhibitors act therapeutically by preventing the breakdown of the neurotransmitters dopamine, norepinephrine, and serotonin. They also prevent the breakdown of tyramine, a constituent of several foods, which is normally broken down in the intestine before being absorbed. When MAOIs prevent such breakdown, tyramine enters the bloodstream, where it can cause a sudden increase in blood pressure, sometimes to a threatening level. If MAOIs raise blood pressure, they do so only briefly. They do not produce hypertension—constant elevated blood pressure.

The MAOIs are very useful agents and are often effective when other antidepressants are not. Hypertension rarely occurs when a patient follows the dietary instructions. When investigators discovered what was producing hypertension and how to prevent it, MAOIs began to be used increasingly in the United States. Because dangerously high blood pressure can be avoided by simple precautions, these effective agents are increasingly used by experienced psychopharmacologists in early-onset depressions marked by overeating, oversleeping, lethargy, and rejection sensitivity (atypical depression).

Side effects.   Low blood pressure and dizziness after standing, sleep disturbances, weight gain, and sexual difficulties occur similar to those seen with the tricyclic antidepressants, SSRIs, and Effexor, and rapid increase in blood pressure produced by eating certain foods or by taking certain medications are among the side effects of this drug group. The sudden rise in blood pressure that may occur with the MAOIs is distinctive in that it causes a severe, throbbing headache localized initially in the back of the head.

Management of side effects.   Many doctors give patients on MAOIs a quick blood-pressure-reducing antidote called nifedipine (Procardia, Adalat). If the patient develops the severe pounding headache that accompanies a sudden increase in blood pressure, he can self-administer this antidote, which quickly lowers the blood pressure to normal. The foods the patient on MAOIs should avoid are those in which there is a large amount of protein fermentation. This particularly applies to all aged cheeses, such as Camembert and Stilton. Every doctor who prescribes MAOIs will provide the patient with a list of foods to avoid. Most patients do not find this diet unduly restrictive.

Anyone who is receiving MAOIs should tell his nonpsychiatrist physician and should check with a pharmacist before taking any other prescribed drug or any over-the-counter drugs (some over-the-counter drugs will raise blood pressure if taken with MAOIs).

As with other antidepressants, other side effects are managed by dose adjustment; the physician attempts to find a dose low enough to control the symptoms without producing the undesired side effects.

Recently, a new class of MAOIs, referred to as *reversible MAOIs*, has been developed. One such drug, moclobemide, does not require dietary restrictions and is currently available abroad. Other similar drugs are being developed. It is likely that these agents will prove popular and useful if they come to the United States market. However, it is possible that concerns about profitability may prevent this.

Desyrel (trazodone)

Trazodone was one of the first of the "new" class of antidepressants. (The only drugs that had been available for years were the tricyclic antidepressants and the monoamine oxidase inhibitors.) It was initially prescribed widely—particularly in suicidal patients who physicians were afraid might overdose—because of its safety. Over the passage of time, most psychiatrists have been disappointed with its effectiveness. For that reason, and because of a bad side effect described below, it is now rarely used as an antidepressant. It is still extremely useful as a "sleeping pill." Even with effective antidepressant treatment, some patients have difficulty falling or staying asleep. Patients usually become tolerant to other sleeping agents and require escalating doses, and may become physically dependent on them. Tolerance to trazodone develops slowly, if at all. However, some patients cannot tolerate the side effects of too much sedation in the morning.

Side effects.   The major disadvantage is that about 1 man in 8,000 who takes the drug may develop "priapism," a prolonged, painful erection of the penis. If this is not treated immediately—by the injection of drugs that terminate the erection—permanent impotence may result. For this reason many psychopharmacologists prefer not to use it in men unless all other treatments are found unsatisfactory.

Mood-Stabilizing Drugs

Lithium

The discovery of the effectiveness of lithium in the treatment of manic-depressive disorder was one of the major psychopharmacological advances of this century; lithium is one of the few "miracle drugs" in psychiatry. Approximately 70 to 80 percent of manic-depressive patients respond very favorably to lithium.

As mentioned earlier, lithium is a metal that is a "close relative" of sodium and potassium, and it is used in the form of a salt, lithium carbonate (just as salt is used in sodium chloride, or table salt). Lithium is used to treat mania, to prevent the recurrence of manic and depressive episodes, and also, in smaller amounts, to increase the effect of antidepressants (in this use it is said to "augment" the effects). The most important aspect of treatment with lithium is a careful adjustment of the dose so that its level in the blood will be within a certain range. Too low a level is ineffective, and too high a level will produce serious side effects. To establish the correct level, the physician begins with a low dose of lithium and waits until the concentration in the blood is stable, slowly increasing the dose until it is within the therapeutic range. To determine the blood level requires periodic blood tests. These should be carried out about 12 hours after the last dose of medication is received. Many physicians find that lithium is best given in a single dose at night rather than being spread out during the day. The frequency with which blood tests are taken depends on where the patient is in the course of treatment. Early in treatment, once or twice a week is sensible because you are not quite sure what a given dose will produce in the way of blood level. After a few months, this should be clear and far less frequent blood tests become necessary.

Side effects.   Minor side effects of lithium may include diarrhea, a metallic taste in the mouth, increased frequency of urination, slight hand tremor, and weight gain.

Two less common side effects require special comment: (1) About 3 percent of patients receiving lithium develop underactivity of the thyroid gland. If lithium treatment is working effectively, the simple and entirely safe remedy is to administer a small amount of thyroid hormone to bring the blood level of the hormone to the correct point. (2) In some patients lithium prevents the kidney from concentrating urine effectively. As a result, those patients must drink more water than usual and will urinate more frequently. This is an annoying side effect, and it is one the physician will monitor. Taking all the lithium in one dose at night decreases this side effect, and medications are available to counteract it.

Tests while taking lithium.   The regular tests employed at intervals of four to six months to monitor lithium treatment include measurement of the lithium blood level, the level of thyroid hormones in the blood, the concentrating ability of the kidney, and kidney function. Although some alterations in kidney function may occur with long-term lithium use, they are never life-threatening; if lithium proves effective, their inconvenience is greatly outweighed by the benefit of the medication.

Precautions.   Some routine precautions are necessary while taking lithium. Lithium is perfectly safe at the right dose, but may be dangerous if its level is allowed to become too high. This risk is entirely preventable by monitoring lithium blood levels and maintaining fluid intake. Early symptoms of excess lithium in the blood are shaking, trembling, feeling confused, vomiting, and diarrhea. These symptoms may be brought on by water loss, which can occur either with intestinal "viruses" that produce severe diarrhea or vomiting or through severe dehydration. Such dehydration can be brought on by high environmental temperatures (as on the beach or in the desert), vigorous exercise, long periods without drinking, or any combination of these. To maintain correct levels of lithium in the blood, the patient should drink approximately six glasses of water a day and not be on a salt-restricted diet. If the patient does develop a "stomach virus" accompanied by diarrhea or vomiting, he should discontinue the lithium immediately, increase his fluid intake, and contact his physician.

The necessity for these precautions should not frighten patients away from the use of lithium. Handled correctly, lithium is as safe as the medications used for high blood pressure or the insulin used in diabetes. Like patients with these disorders, the lithium patient rapidly learns the precautions and danger signals.

Anticonvulsants

For unknown reasons, some manic patients who respond only partially to treatment with lithium, or lithium and neuroleptics, respond to treatment with lithium combined with certain anti-convulsant drugs.

Tegretol (carbamazepine)

Carbamazepine was the first anticonvulsant drug found effective when added to lithium in partially responsive manic-depressive patients. As with lithium, the dosage of carbamazepine must be adjusted on an individual basis; as the dose is increased, further tests must be done to ensure that the proper blood level has been reached (too little is ineffective, but too much may be toxic).

Side effects. The side effects here include dizziness, drowsiness, unsteadiness, and mental cloudiness. For these reasons some patients cannot tolerate the drug. A rare serious side effect occurs in about 1 patient in 50,000: in these patients Tegretol interferes with the body's production of blood cells, which can be life threatening if allowed to persist. Accordingly, the routine blood tests that are administered when treatment is started are especially important, and the medication must be discontinued if abnormalities develop. Some psychopharmacologists suggest that blood tests should be obtained weekly or twice weekly during the first two or three months, and approximately every three months thereafter. However, there is considerable controversy about this; some psychopharmacologists recommend more frequent and others less frequent testing.

Depakote (divalproex)

This anticonvulsant drug is often used for the treatment of epilepsy. Like Tegretol, it is generally added when a manic patient has responded only partially to lithium. It is begun at low levels, and the dose is kept constant for a few days while the blood level is measured. The dosage of medication is then gradually increased until it is within the therapeutic range. Depakote has proved a particularly successful mood stabilizer. Many psychopharmacologists will use it without lithium, especially in atypical cases of mania or rapid cycling cases.

Side effects.   Among the side effects are drowsiness, weight gain, and hair loss, which sometimes occur initially. One major precaution may be indicated in the use of these drugs. They have been used in severely epileptic infants who were receiving other anticonvulsants, and some developed liver damage. Although no liver damage has been reported in adults receiving Depakote, as a precautionary measure, some physicians check liver function at periodic intervals by blood testing.

In some bipolar patients, anticonvulsants alone may control the symptoms. Both anticonvulsants have proved valuable agents in manic-depressive patients who respond only partially to treatment with lithium, neuroleptics, and antidepressants.

Depakote has been found by many patients to be even more easily tolerated than lithium, and many biological psychiatrists are turning to it as the drug of choice in the treatment of manic-depressive illness. It's of interest that it also appears to be helpful in patients with very unstable and explosive moods, or whose moods shift very rapidly between depression and mania. Unfortunately, it is not as well established as lithium as a long-term prophylactic agent.

Lamictal (lamotrigine)

This is an anticonvulsant drug that has been used in the treatment of manic-depression. There is some evidence that it may be effective in treating bipolar patients who are depressed without producing an "overshoot," causing depression to switch into mania.

Side effects.   Lamictal produces rashes, but if started at a very low dose—for example 12.5 mg a day—and raised slowly, this decreases the risk. If medication is discontinued immediately when a rash develops, the rash usually disappears. However, some rashes become serious and require hospitalization, since these rashes may evolve into a serious skin disorder from which death has occurred. The risk of serious rashes is estimated to be 3 in 1,000. But the risk of death is too rare to allow a precise estimate. Other side effects are headache, nausea, dizziness, unsteadiness, and double vision.

Topamax (topiramate)

Topamax is an anticonvulsant that has been used to treat bipolar disorder. Experience with it is limited. It has been employed largely because it does not produce weight gain and may produce weight loss.

Side effects.   Side effects occur in a large number of patients. These include fatigue, dizziness, language facility problems, and the development of a "pins and needles" sensation in the body. Other symptoms include sleepiness, mental slowing, and difficulties with focusing attention. These side effects are often confused with depression. This drug requires a cautious approach and close monitoring.

Newer Anticonvulsants

Other anticonvulsant drugs are reported to be effective in manic-depression. These include zonisamide (Zonegram), tiagasine (Gabatril), and oxicarbazepine (Trileptal). Clinical experience is too limited to accurately determine the effectiveness of these drugs.

Neuroleptics

Neuroleptics, also called antipsychotics, were the first drugs effective in the treatment of schizophrenia, the psychosis most often associated with "insanity." This illness is still the area of their major use, but they have also proved helpful in two forms of mood disorder. First, they are useful in the treatment of excited manic patients. When patients are very excited, the combination of neuroleptics and lithium works faster than lithium alone. The neuroleptics can generally be discontinued (while lithium is continued) when the manic patient achieves normal mood. The other use of neuroleptics is with depressed patients who are very agitated. Such patients may suffer from inner feelings of great anxiety and a constant urge to move. These unpleasant symptoms are more effectively relieved by neuroleptics than by tranquilizers such as Ativan.

Side effects.   When neuroleptics are administered in large doses for long periods of time, they may produce alterations in neurological functioning called *tardive dyskinesia*, which is characterized by repetitive, involuntary movement. These abnormalities are often reversible if the neuroleptics are discontinued. Since treatment of mood disorders with neuroleptics is necessary with only a few manic-depressive patients and agitated depressive patients, and is usually brief in those instances, the risks that accompany high-dose, long-term administration are minimal. However, should the use of neuroleptics seem advisable, the physician should discuss the potential risks and benefits with the patient or the patient's family.

Atypical Antipsychotics

Zyprexa (olanzapine), Risperdal (risperidone),
Seroquel (quetiapine), Geodon (ziprasidone)

The atypical antipsychotics are a group of novel drugs that were developed to treat psychosis and produce fewer neurological side effects. Of them, Clozaril (clozapine) is outstanding as often improving the status of patients with schizophrenia who have only partially (or not at all) responded to classical antipsychotics. The problem with this medication is that it may infrequently produce a fatal blood disorder, agranulocytosis. Therefore, it is definitely not a first choice medication. Depressed patients who have responded only partially to antidepressants may experience improvements when atypical antipsychotics are added. Atypical antipsychotics have also been found useful in the treatment of severe mania, often producing improvement more rapidly than lithium and the anticonvulsants.

Side effects.   Although they produce fewer neurological side effects than the neuroleptics, the atypical antipsychotics do produce them in some patients. In these patients, there is the risk that long-term treatment may produce permanent neurological changes. The risk of neurological side effects differs among these drugs. Another side effect, more pronounced in some than in others, is increased weight. Similarly, some are more likely to produce metabolic changes when used for some period of time. Common side effects are sedation, increased appetite, dry mouth, and lowered blood pressure. Much remains to be learned about their utility for mood disorders.

Minor Tranquilizers: Benzodiazepines

Benzodiazepines (BZDs) are the common tranquilizers whose brand names—Valium and Ativan—have entered our popular language. The several kinds of BZDs on the market differ mainly in how rapidly they induce calmness after they are taken, and how long their effects last. The duration of effectiveness of different BZDs ranges from hours to weeks. Making allowances for their different strengths, all are equally effective, and they are often useful in the treatment of acute anxiety in depressives. Alprazolam (Xanax) and clonazepam (Klonopin), which are very close relatives of the traditional benzodiazepines, have special utility in the treatment of panic disorder. Unlike the drugs mentioned previously, benzodiazepines can be abused. However, most of their abuse has occurred in alcoholics; accordingly, great care must be used when these drugs are prescribed to treat alcoholics.

A problem with the benzodiazepines is that, when they are administered for prolonged periods of time, the body may adjust to them and become "dependent" on them. If the benzodiazepines are then abruptly withdrawn, individuals may suffer symptoms of agitation and anxiety. Dependence can be avoided by using benzodiazepines in as low doses as possible, for as short a period as possible, and by decreasing the dose gradually when they are being withdrawn. However, for patients with chronic anxiety, chronic administration may be necessary.

Side effects.   The major side effect of this drug group is drowsiness, which generally disappears with time. A few people become slightly confused, especially with higher doses. And a few patients taking BZDs experience memory deficits, which requires close monitoring by the physician.

There had been media concern about Halcion, a potent, short-acting benzodiazepine that has been widely used for the treatment of insomnia. The problem is that Halcion, on occasion, produces a peculiar phenomenon called *anterograde amnesia*. One may take a dose of Halcion at night, wake up in the morning, carry on the activities of the morning, and then in the afternoon remember nothing about the morning's activities. From what we now know, Halcion seems to interfere with the laying down of recent events into long-term memory when taken in high doses. In carrying out life's activities, this side effect is an annoyance and may even be frightening, but it does not interfere with one's daily functioning. The distinction between short-term memory and long-term memory is of great current interest to those trying to understand how our mind works, but an explanation of this baffling side effect is still beyond our reach.

Does Halcion represent a substantial risk? The United Kingdom has banned Halcion but the United States has not. Who is correct? Clearly, we would like to rely on good scientific data, but there is not a great deal to go on. What is clear is that risk depends largely on the dosage taken. Our belief is that low doses of Halcion—that is, one-eighth to one-quarter mg for sleep—are probably useful for short-term treatment of the vast majority of people and only very occasionally problematic, with regard to memory, for a small percentage of the population. The Halcion controversy is another example of how tracking patients on newly released drugs after FDA approval would clearly be in the public interest.

Newer Sleeping Agents

Two new sleeping agents are Ambien (zolpidem) and Sonata (zaleplon). These drugs act quickly and may wear off after three to four hours in the early morning hours. If taken for periods of more than one month, patients may become tolerant and require increasing doses. After repeated use, the patient may find it difficult to fall asleep without using these agents.

Herbal Remedies

The FDA evaluates new drugs and assesses their purity, effectiveness, and side effects in treatment of particular conditions. In contrast, herbal remedies are not screened by the FDA and are available over the counter. The reason herbal remedies have not been screened by the FDA is because Congress permits their sale as "nutritional supplements" without evaluation for safety and efficacy. There are therefore almost no comparisons of herbal remedies with established treatments and no evaluation of the nature and frequency of their side effects. Being "natural" does not mean a substance is safe. In fact, these drugs evolved in plants to make them bad tasting or poisonous. Morphine, used to treat pain, and digitalis, used to treat heart failure, are both derived from plants and are both lethal in overdose.

The herbal remedy reputed to be an effective antidepressant is St. John's Wort. St. John's Wort has been compared to placebo in the treatment of moderate and severe depression. The findings were that St. John's Wort was no more effective in relieving depression than placebo.

Some people have said that although St. John's Wort may be ineffective in more severe depressions, it is more effective than placebo in treating mild depressions. Only when such a study is conducted will we know if this is true. Being ineffective in the treatment of moderate depression does not mean that it is free of side effects. In particular, if a patient taking St. John's Wort is treated with an SSRI, he or she may develop a severe toxic reaction. The frequency of other side effects of St. John's Wort is not known, nor its safety when taken over an extended period of time.

Another popular herb, Ephedra, was just banned by the FDA for safety concerns.

Monitoring Drug Treatment

There is a complicated issue with regard to the biological monitoring of medication through the use of laboratory procedures. Some biological psychiatrists believe that, by closely monitoring the blood level, they can achieve the best trade-off between safety and effectiveness. Other, equally informed biological psychiatrists believe that these careful measurements are generally not helpful and that, in fact, the relationship between the blood level of a drug and the effective level of the drug in that part of the brain where it works is probably rather poor. Thus, it would be surprising if such blood measures were of great benefit. In general, the measuring of blood levels is primarily for safety rather than efficacy. For instance, measuring the blood level of lithium and the anticonvulsants is important because it can get too high and produce toxicity. To avoid this, we need to observe blood levels. However, for only very few other psychiatric drugs has it been shown that monitoring blood levels avoids toxicity. Also, for very few drugs has it been shown that some minimal blood level is necessary before you can be assured that the medication will do its job.

What is the patient to do? Our suggestion is that the informed, skilled biological psychiatrist is most likely to make sense of confusing data and controversial findings. Your best chance of arriving at a reasonable conclusion is by working with someone who knows the pros and cons of the arguments.

7

Illnesses Related to Depression

THE FOUR SECTIONS of this chapter deal with panic disorder, which involves a set of symptoms that frequently accompanies depression, and three varieties of depressive illness.

Panic and Depression

We are including a discussion of panic disorder in this book because it is often found in patients with depression. In addition, patients who experience both panic disorder and depression often have substantially more difficulty in overcoming their illness than those who are only depressed. A special problem is that for such sufferers, panic attacks and their accompanying chronic anxiety, which we describe below, frequently are the major complaints. Because most such patients focus on their severe attacks of anxiety, many physicians treat them with minor tranquilizers such as Valium, which are ineffective in the treatment of panic disorder and depression. Antidepressant medication, however, is effective for both panic and depression.

Therefore, recognizing that a patient has panic disorder can set him or her on the right treatment road.

Panic, like *depression*, is a confusing word for most people because it is part of common speech. One often hears people who are upset, who are feeling overwhelmed or are thinking of a difficult future task, say that they are "panicky."

When psychiatrists use the term *panic disorder*, they do not mean ordinary feelings of being anxious or upset but rather a particular sudden explosion—a crescendo—of physical symptoms, usually but not always accompanied by great fear. The outstanding physical symptoms are heart pounding, shortness of breath, trembling, a sudden fear of impending death or insanity, and an intense urge to flee. Of special note are the sudden onset, which peaks within a few minutes, and the relatively short duration. Some patients say that their panic lasts for hours, but they are usually referring to the feeling of fright that follows the initial panic. That feeling lasts, but the initial fast heartbeat, shortness of breath, and so on, subside quickly.

Another distinguishing feature of the panic attack is that it often occurs for no obvious reason. The person may be quietly walking down the street when she is suddenly struck with an attack. Such panics are referred to as spontaneous panics. Their identification is very important because they have a specific medical treatment.

People who have panic attacks usually think they have suddenly become frightened for no apparent reason. Although much psychological theory has looked on the panic attack as sudden fear, we do not consider it the same as ordinary fear. There are marked similarities, such as trembling and sweating, but the kind of fear that occurs in armed combat is only infrequently marked by shortness of breath, which occurs in almost all spontaneous panics. Furthermore, hormones such as adrenalin and cortisone, which are normally released during emergencies, are not released during spontaneous panic. We are pointing out such differences in order to help in the recognition of panic attacks. Once identified, this illness is one of the most treatable of disorders.

Occasional panic *attacks* are probably fairly common. It has been estimated that 20 to 30 percent of the population have them once in a while. Panic *disorder*, however, consists of the regular repetition of spontaneous panic attacks. If a person has had one attack a week for three or four weeks, he probably has panic disorder. If he has had only one severe attack but has been thrown into a state of persistent, apprehensive worry about when the next panic will occur, that, too, may be panic disorder.

Some patients with panic disorder seem able to go about their business without undue worry that the panic may recur or with a feeling of resignation—they believe that if it does recur, they can withstand it. Others, after several panics, rush to emergency rooms, develop chronic apprehension, and eventually start avoiding situations where they could not easily get help if a panic suddenly occurred. They also begin to avoid places where they had a panic attack. If a panic occurred at a supermarket, they avoid the supermarket; if at a church, they avoid the church. The panics are not produced by being in these places, but when the first attack occurs in a specific situation, they *learn* to avoid that situation. These people begin to avoid driving through tunnels or over bridges, being in a strange neighborhood, or being alone. Their travel frequently becomes substantially restricted. They may spend more and more time at home, and some will not venture out without a companion. If they have to go somewhere—for example, to church—they experience anxiety when anticipating the return to a place where they experienced a panic attack. They have been psychologically conditioned. In the extreme, they become housebound. Patients with marked life restrictions because of fear of panic are called *agoraphobic*. For panic-prone patients whose lives are constricted in some of these ways, demoralization can be severe.

The following illustrative case narratives have been used in training therapists in a research study of the treatment of panic attacks.

■ *Edna Elie* was a 25-year-old woman who had been living and working in Manhattan for four years since college graduation. She recalls having symptoms of anxiety as a child, and at that time she was terrified of being in cars, where she experienced heart palpitations and fear of loss of control. She attributed her anxiety to the sensation of speed or rapid motion, and also disliked swings and amusement park rides.

Nonetheless, as an adult, Edna became a proficient driver. However, at age 23 she experienced her first spontaneous panic attack while driving a car. It came out of the blue, and she experienced feelings of terror and shortness of breath. Sine the feelings were short lived, she dismissed the experience and put it out of her mind. A month later Edna and her boyfriend broke up, and shortly afterward she had a second spontaneous panic, again while driving a car. This time her symptoms were worse. She had a rush of terror, difficulty in breathing, palpitations and chest discomfort; she felt light-headed and flushed; and she feared that she would faint, that she was going crazy, and that she was losing control She had to pull over to the side of the road and have a family member take over.

In the following month Edna began to have attacks every week. Since she was now also having them in buses and subways, she had to take taxis to work.

Two months later, Edna and her boyfriend reunited, started living together, and got engaged. At about the same time, her father had heart surgery. Shortly thereafter, she began to have several attacks every day, mostly "out of the blue," and even at home and at work. Eventually she had to quit her job. She became fearful of going out at all but forced herself to do so.

After some months, Edna began to feel less energetic, less interested in activities, more unresponsive to potential rewards. Every day became an increasing burden so that she felt unable to even attempt to look for work.

This case is typical in many ways, First, the subject is a woman, and women are distinctly more prone to experience panic attacks than men. Second, she had had a period of anxiety as a child. That appears to be true for roughly half the women who develop panic attacks in later life. Most frequently, the childhood anxiety centers around the fear of separation from the mother, often appearing as a refusal to go to school—a symptom that this patient did not recall. The course of her illness, however, is again quite typical, with the onset coming unexpectedly but seemingly made worse by the threat of important personal losses. It is also typical that following severe life constriction and continuing panic the patient becomes demoralized in the sense of becoming severely pessimistic and unresponsive to usual interests and pleasures.

■ *Tim Thompson* was a 26-year-old, single, male high school teacher who lived alone. He had his first panic attack while routinely preparing for his class one morning. He felt dizzy, had difficulty breathing, and had an unusual feeling that things around him did not look quite real. The feelings of unreality lasted for about an hour. Over the next several months he developed weekly episodes, primarily but not always on the morning of a school day. Typically his head would swim, he felt distant from what was going on, he had difficulty breathing and some chest pain, and he feared that he might be having a heart attack.

He went to several physicians, and all tests were negative. One physician told him that he was having panic attacks and stated that medication might be useful. He was relieved that he did not have a heart condition but refused a prescription because he did not like the idea of taking medicine. He then stopped drinking his regular two cups of strong coffee in the morning, which resulted in his feeling less anxious. The panic attacks persisted but were less frequent and less severe. Tim was still plagued by the idea that he might have a heart attack, but he continued to work efficiently, did not have much anticipatory anxiety between episodes, and did not avoid traveling.

Tim always maintained his ability to enjoy himself and to pursue his interests. He continued to worry about his heart, but did not feel fatalistic.

This patient also shows a number of typical features. First, Time followed the pattern seen in men, who are somewhat less likely than women to develop the phobias (fear of being alone, of going out by oneself, etc.). Second, he had caffeine sensitivity. Although his morning coffees were probably not the entire cause of his panic, clearly they had made matters worse. Third, Tim viewed his symptoms as physical in origin but was eventually able to gain some reassurance from medical examinations that revealed no serious illness. Finally, he resisted taking medication for his condition, a common reaction of patients when psychological symptoms cannot be traced to specific physical malfunctions. Tim did not become depressed, which indicated that panic disorder is not simply a variation of depression but rather a related condition.

■   *Linda Light*, a 38-year-old woman who worked as a hairdresser, had her first panic attack at age 33 while at work. One morning she experienced a sudden, unexplained onset of fear, accompanied by shortness of breath, palpitations, chest pain, a choking feeling, dizziness, hot flashes, faintness, nausea, trembling, fear of dying, and fear of losing control. She thought she was having a heart attack. These feelings went away in about a half hour but recurred later that morning. Co-workers drove her to a physician, who examined her thoroughly and said that all tests were negative, and therefore prescribed Valium. The panics continued several times a week, but Linda took the Valium irregularly, usually waiting until after she had had a panic attack. Her attacks began to appear in a somewhat less severe fashion, but she worried about them continuously.

About three months after her first attacks, Linda became pregnant. She was panic free during her pregnancy. For the first few years after her daughter was born, she had infrequent attacks—about three or four a year—and they were not very severe, consisting of brief periods of fearfulness, heart palpitations, and dizziness. She would forget about them shortly after they were over.

Linda was considering starting work on a part-time basis and having her mother take care of her little girl when her attacks came back in full force on a daily basis. Some were relatively minor, but others were as severe as the first panics. She sometimes felt so overwhelmed that it took several hours to recover from the exhaustion and fear that she experienced. Since she felt that she could not give in to her symptoms and had to keep the house running, she forced herself to shop and carry on other activities. However, she cut down her social activities and felt unable to return to her work as a hairdresser; she was afraid of having an attack while cutting hair and not being able to explain what was happening to her.

Linda's mood varied. At times, when playing with her daughter, she felt perfectly content and happy. At other times, when thinking of going back to work, she felt overwhelmed, despairing, and pessimistic.

This case also has several typical features. Again, the initial attack "appeared from nowhere," and the patient developed fears of a heart attack despite a negative medical workup. A mild tranquilizer was prescribed and was only slightly helpful. The patient lost her symptoms during pregnancy, and that is typical. This indicates to us that there may be a physiological basis for the panic attack and that pregnancy provides an antidote. Interestingly, women are also panic free during the period of breastfeeding.

The flare-up in Linda's panic attacks may have been related to her plans to separate herself from her daughter. She also developed social phobias—that is, fear of being embarrassed or humiliated in case she were to have a panic attack while working. She did not become agoraphobic, and could endure travel even though she dreaded it.

Note that Linda's periods of pessimistic despair could easily be misunderstood as biological depression. This is of some importance because some antidepressants do not benefit panic disorder and some antipanic agents do not benefit depression. Therefore, it is extremely important to determine if a patient has panic disorder, depression, or both illnesses.

The Nature of Panic Disorder

In explaining panic disorder, some people emphasize biological causes for the attacks, while others emphasize a psychological origin. The psychological explanation is that some people develop an uncomfortable physical sensation, misinterpret it as dangerous, and frighten themselves into an attack. Once having done this, they perceive similar sensations as even more dangerous, leading to a vicious circle and recurrent attacks.

Our view is that although the vicious circle may make panics worse, it is unlikely that this is the cause of the attacks, because some patients have panics while asleep or while relaxing under safe circumstances, and women are not likely to have panics during pregnancy or breastfeeding. The rareness of panics during pregnancy seems especially significant because pregnancy is the source of many distressing internal sensations that could easily be misinterpreted as dangerous. However, we agree with a psychological explanation for the development of phobias that develop *after* repeated panic attacks—the learned or conditioned phobias we have just discussed. Our experience with the drug treatment of panic attacks strengthens our view of these separate causes, as we will explain.

In the early 1960s one of us (DFK) discovered that the antidepressant imipramine (Tofranil) prevented the occurrence of panic attacks. However, it did not relieve the fears that developed as a result of the panic attacks—fears of driving, of leaving the house, and so forth. The fact that imipramine had knocked out the most serious form of anxiety without affecting the chronic (and learned) anticipatory anxiety indicated that these anxieties probably had two different causes. The older psychological theories about anxiety and panic reasoned that a patient becomes increasingly anxious until he is finally overwhelmed by anxiety. But as the case histories show, the chronic anxiety occurs after—not before—the panic attacks. The patient is usually feeling reasonably well, although perhaps under some stress, when a spontaneous panic attack occurs. After repeated attacks, chronic anxiety develops.

By now there are several useful medications for spontaneous panic attacks. Interestingly, these medications do not work for the person who has what is called a specific phobia. In a *specific phobia*, a particular object or situation brings on the panicky feelings. Common examples are fears of insects or snakes. A person with spider phobia suddenly confronted with a spider may have a wave of terror and suddenly dash away. Because this kind of triggered panic is not benefited by imipramine, it is important to distinguish between spontaneous panics and other suddenly provoked fearful experiences. Simple phobias are often benefited by behavioral treatment— in particular, *exposure therapy*. In this treatment, the patient is successfully brought closer and closer to the phobic object with repeated demonstrations that she is not actually in any danger and that she can master her fears.

Treatment with Antidepressants

Extensive clinical experience with various tricyclic antidepressants and SSRIs indicates that they probably all work on panic attacks. As we said earlier, tricyclic antidepressants are safe and effective. Monoamine oxidase inhibitors (MAOIs) are also extremely effective in the treatment of panic disorder, but the possible side effects require special cautions.

Drugs such as Ativan are widely used for the relief of chronic anxiety and reactions to illness, but they are not particularly effective against panic. However, two "high-potency benzodiazepines" have been found to be effective against panic— alprazolam (Xanax) and clonazepam (Klonopin). These drugs have several distinct advantages and one substantial disadvantage. They are quicker to work than the other medications. One often sees marked benefits within the first week, whereas the other medications will take from three to six weeks to work. They have exceptionally few side effects, and most patients can easily tolerate them, except for some sedative effects at times. The substantial difficulty is that they produce a physical dependence so that the patient cannot go off the medication abruptly. The dosage must be lowered slowly under a doctor's supervision. During this period there is frequently a recurrence of anxiety symptoms, and relapse may occur after the medication is stopped. It is not clear whether the relapse is temporary or permanent. Nonetheless, for patients who cannot tolerate tricyclic antidepressants and do not want to run the risk of monoamine oxidase inhibitors, these agents are tremendously helpful.

Fluoxetine (Prozac) has comparatively few side effects when used in the treatment of depression and is tolerated well. However, about half the patients with panic disorder are markedly hypersensitive to Prozac. They react to the usual starting dose of 20 mg as if they have been given a very strong stimulant. A common patient response is "I feel as if I'm jumping out of my skin." This response is also seen in about 10 to 15 percent of the patients treated with tricyclic antidepressants, but it is more severe and more frequent with Prozac. We have therefore initiated the practice of starting patients with panic disorder at the level of 2.5 mg daily (one-eighth of the usual starting dose). We then slowly raise the dose by small increments to a level that can control the panics with minimal side effects.

There are as yet no systematic studies of Prozac in the treatment of panic disorder, but our own experience with it convinces us that, in patients who can tolerate it, there are excellent antipanic effects within four to six weeks.

Zoloft, in initial doses of 25 mg daily, is well tolerated by most panic patients and appears effective, as is Paxil in doses of 10 mg daily.

Given all these options, which medications should be used? We believe that the doctor and the patient should discuss the pros and cons of each treatment. The informed patient should be the one to make the decision as to which medication to use, or whether to use a medication at all. However, most people who refuse medication do so on the basis of unrealistic anxiety; it is the doctor's task to help the patient to become fully informed about the benefits and risks of the medications.

Treatment with Psychotherapy

Once a physical examination has ruled out a medical origin of panic symptoms, the question arises: can panic attacks and agoraphobia be treated by psychological methods, thus making it unnecessary to use medication? Before the effects of antidepressants were discovered, the most common psychological treatment for agoraphobia was exposure therapy.

Exposure therapy is a *behavior therapy* in which the patient gradually relearns to leave her home—that is, to return to the feared situation. First, she is encouraged to walk outside for a short distance—say, to the corner—often with the therapist. As she grows more at ease, she tries longer excursions—around the block or to a nearby park. Eventually, she can resume taking buses and visiting neighborhood shops. Finally, she can again travel alone.

A number of studies have shown that exposure therapy is effective in decreasing the patient's *phobic avoidance*—that is, the patient no longer avoids the world outside the "safe" home ground. However, our own and other studies indicate that, while the phobic avoidance has decreased, the panic attacks remain. The patients learn to become stoical about the panic—they learn to endure it. Instead of running home or to an emergency room when they get a panic, they now understand that the panic attack is harmless, even though very upsetting; many patients can learn just to sit down and wait for the attack to go away, and then resume whatever they were doing. In our view, exposure therapy is not a treatment for panic disorder but a treatment for the phobias that develop as a result of panic disorder. However, once the panic attacks have been controlled by medication, exposure therapy helps the patient to unlearn her learned phobias. Now that she no longer experiences attacks, she will overcome her phobias more quickly if she returns to supermarkets, bridges, and other panic-inducing situations, and "deconditions" herself—that is, learns through experience that panics do not occur in these places. She may also learn this through ordinary experience, but learning through exposure therapy may be considerably faster.

Recently, a behavior therapy for panic attacks has been developed in which the patient is purposely exposed to situations in which panic-like symptoms develop—but under controlled circumstances. For example, patients are given certain demanding physical exercises or rotated dizzyingly in chairs until an increased heart rate, breathlessness, and nausea mimic their panic symptoms. This procedure is repeated until the patients learn not to overreact to these symptoms. These treatments are frequently combined with a cognitive approach to the panic in which the patient is trained to understand that the symptoms are harmless and that the fearful reactions are unnecessary; this therapy also supports a stoical attitude. Researchers claim that this technique reduces the number of panics and even produces cures. Unfortunately, systematic evidence for effectiveness has only been found in patients with pure panic disorder, who have not become phobic.

One particularly interesting feature of the behavioral approaches to panic is training in slow, shallow breathing. This is usually done with the aid of a relaxation tape. If the patient suffers only from occasional spontaneous panics, does not have any of the phobic complications, and recognizes that she is in no serious danger, then learning how to breathe shallowly at the rate of 10 to 12 breaths per minute, and doing that for 20 minutes twice a day, may be useful. As usual, this is denied by some experts.

Atypical Depression

As we indicated earlier in the book, typical depression is usually characterized by a widespread inability to enjoy life in any way, marked insomnia, and loss of appetite.

However, researchers have gradually realized that some patients with contrasting symptoms also suffer from depression. They respond positively to good things that happen to them, they are able to enjoy simple pleasures like food and sex, and they tend to oversleep and overeat. Their depression, which is chronic rather than periodic and that usually dates from adolescence, largely shows itself in lack of energy and interest, lack of initiative, and a great sensitivity to episodic—particularly romantic—rejection by others. Some of these patients also have occasional spontaneous panics. Extensive studies have shown that atypical depression is common. Individuals with this disorder do not respond well to tricyclic antidepressants, but they do very well on monoamine oxidase inhibitors. This is surprising because in "typical depression" both types of antidepressants work well. A case illustration follows. The earlier the onset and the more chronic the disorder, the more likely that only MAOIs will be helpful.

■ *Barbara Bahm* was a 44-year-old woman who arrived for treatment complaining of chronic depression since early childhood. Her longest period of well-being had been during her pregnancy and the year after the birth of her first child. She had a similar period of well-being after the birth of her second child.

The major symptom accompanying her depression was constant lethargy, with a feeling of leaden heaviness. She frequently overslept by several hours and spent a great deal of time in bed. She tends to overeat when depressed and had gained ten pounds in the last year. She does not eat regular meals, but picks at a variety of junk foods throughout the day. Although only ten pounds over her ideal body weight, she felt quite obese.

Barbara's mood is clearly affected by favorable events, and she can enjoy a good party. She is sensitive to rejection and says that feeling rejected makes her angry and depressed. Her tendency to react in that way has lessened over the years but initially strained her marriage.

Barbara had a spontaneous panic attack at about age 11, associated with typical symptoms. Panic attacks have recurred irregularly since then. However, she has not developed agoraphobia. She believes her mother was also chronically depressed, although the details are not clear, and she believes that her son, now age 20, has symptoms similar to hers. Extensive psychotherapy earlier in her life decreased some of her interpersonal and vocational difficulties, but did not relieve her depression or anxiety. Under her doctor's care, she tried 150 mg of imipramine, over a few weeks, some years ago without benefit and was currently taking Valium with moderate benefit.

Barbara responded well to treatment with Nardil (an MAOI), becoming energetic, losing weight, and getting along better with her husband. The panics also ceased. After six months, she discontinued medication but relapsed quickly. Returning to medication, she once again felt normal.

This patient's symptoms are characteristic of atypical depression—chronic lethargy, sensitivity to rejection, overeating, oversleeping, and sporadic panic attacks. That she dates her depression from childhood is somewhat unusual since most such patients date their depression from adolescence. Her lack of response to imipramine (a tricyclic) and positive response to Nardil (a MAOI) are also customary.

Since Prozac is a simpler drug to use than Nardil, many patients with atypical depression are first treated with Prozac. Recent experience indicates that even if Prozac appears successful, these gains are rarely maintained. Also, its use requires a five-week delay before switching to a MAOI.

Seasonal Affective Disorder

One kind of depressive illness that closely resembles atypical depression is seasonal affective disorder. Patients with this disorder commonly develop symptoms much like those of atypical depression but only during the periods of the year with less daylight. They regularly cheer up during the summer. Of great interest is the fact that exposure to bright light in the morning, which has the effect of extending the day, has a quick beneficial effect on many such patients. Monoamine oxidase inhibitors also help seasonal affective disorder. An example of a patient with such a pattern follows.

■ *Claire Cooper*, a 31-year-old, single, freelance art director, complained of depression, increased appetite, weight gain, increased sleep duration, low energy, and inactivity beginning in late November each year and lasting through February. Although she first noticed a connection between the time of year and these problems only a few years ago, she remembers that even as a young girl she thought of winter as "dark and scary."

Irritability is a problem for Claire at any time of the year, but she finds herself avoiding company in winter because she feels less tolerant and does not want to snap at people.

During such periods she is still able to concentrate while reading books, but she has more difficulty finding one that she wants to read. She spends most days sitting, sleeping, and watching TV, and frequently does not get out of the apartment all day. When she is at her worst during the winter, she may sleep 14 hours a day. Because of her increase in appetite, particularly for sweets, ice cream, and candy bars, she has put on from 25 to 40 pounds during some winters. Normally, during the summer she loses some or all of the extra pounds gained.

Claire has been in therapy several times, starting in the fall and stopping in the summer when she felt better. When she heard about phototherapy (bright light treatments), she entered an experimental program that consisted of sitting at a desk from six to eight o'clock in the morning, reading the newspaper or doing her work while exposed to a bank of bright lights. Within a week she rapidly responded to the treatment. The change was very distinct, with a marked rise in energy and a decrease in sleep and appetite. She was able to discontinue the light therapy as the amount of natural daylight reached the point where her mood would usually start to improve each spring.

It seems clear that seasonal affective disorder is a biological illness that, in about half the cases, can be benefited by light therapy. We are still learning about this disorder. Its symptoms of oversleeping and overeating closely resemble the symptoms of atypical depression, already described. Our work has shown that light therapy is ineffective for patients with atypical depression who do not have a seasonal pattern. On the other hand, the monoamine oxidase inhibitors, which are effective for atypical depression, are usually effective for seasonal affective disorder. That there are effective treatments is clear.

Premenstrual Syndrome

Women who are thought to have *premenstrual syndrome* (PMS) develop a sudden, sharp, unpleasant change in their emotional state and behavior premenstrually. They are distinguished from women with an enduring depression by the fact that, when their menstrual period ends each month, their mood returns to normal. Prior to their next menstrual period, the same set of symptoms recurs. The symptoms of premenstrual disorder differ substantially from woman to woman. Patients often focus on their mood disturbance—for example, becoming irritable, angry and impatient, depressed, sad, low, blue, lonely, anxious, jittery, and nervous. They may also stay home and avoid social activity. Some patients complain of physical discomfort, including abdominal pain, breast pain, lessened sexual interest, back, joint, or muscle pain, and feelings of being bloated or having edema. Other patients emphasize decreased energy: they sleep longer, take more naps, work less, and feel tired and weak. Another group of premenstrual patients develop a craving for stimulants (amphetamine), and they may actually have more sexual interest, greater activity, and increased efficiency. Excellent studies by Jean Endicott and her co-workers have helped to clear up this confused field by meticulous attention to detail. They emphasize recurrent premenstrual problematic states. It is a mistake to talk about one premenstrual disorder. However, there are various patterns of premenstrual changes that are distressing and may cause impaired functioning.

One problem with this description is that the symptoms do not recur with every cycle, and for some women, the premenstrual emotional unpleasantness occurs irregularly. Clearly, this produced difficulties for those studying the treatment of PMS. For example, if one were studying patients who had irregular PMS and who had just experienced a bad premenstrual episode, it would be quite likely that, at their next period, they would be feeling much better. Therefore, if these patients were then divided into two groups, with one group receiving medication and the other receiving placebo (a sugar pill) before their next period, the placebo group would do as well as the medication group. Until recently, this was exactly what happened in studies of PMS. Most studies failed to show that medication was more effective than placebo because so many women with PMS had "good" months. If they were on placebo they might feel better than the patients on antidepressants because they had no side effects. In some studies 80 percent of the patients receiving drug or placebo did well.

However, better recent studies have required that the diagnosis be established by daily ratings across at least two menstrual cycles. Furthermore, the studies required that for a diagnosis of premenstrual syndrome the symptoms had to be associated with at least moderate social or occupational impairment during most menstrual cycles of the previous year. Most crucially, the daily ratings of symptoms had to demonstrate the absence of significant symptoms for at least one week postmenstrually. In studies using this strict definition, a variety of medications have been shown to be useful, including nortriptyline, alprazolam, and fluoxetine. It appears that fluoxetine—and probably the other effective SSRIs—need be given only during the second half of the menstrual cycle.

One of the difficulties about research and diagnosis in this area is that women with chronic depressive complaints often claim that they have premenstrual syndrome for two reasons. First, they have an increase in their symptoms premenstrually. Second, PMS has tended to be acceptable while depression has been an illness that has not yet come out of the closet. However, these patients are really no different from women who have only chronic depressive disorder. They have similar responses to antidepressant treatment, and with successful treatment, both the chronic depression and the premenstrual syndrome disappear.

In general, women who have premenstrual syndrome without another psychiatric illness have much milder symptoms than patients who have both chronic mood disorder and pre-menstrual syndrome. However, some women have no emotional disorder, yet do have distinct and severe changes in mood, behavior, and functioning during the premenstrual period. It is evident that women who think they may have a premenstrual disorder deserve a complete psychiatric evaluation that is not simply focused on their premenstrual symptoms.

It is also clear that most women do not have a problem with premenstrual changes. However, patients who do have depressive swings in the premenstrual period are particularly prone to develop depressions in later life. Therefore, women should not shrug off a developing depression as simply the result of their menstrual cycle. Instead, like women with severe premenstrual symptoms, they should have an evaluation by a professional skilled in the diagnosis of depression.

8

How to Get Help

ONE OF THE CONFUSING problems that a person with a depression or related illness faces is finding the right kind of therapist. Because therapy for various kinds of emotional disorders is offered not only by psychiatrists but also by psychologists, social workers, nurses, and pastoral counselors, it is difficult for the potential patient to decide who can best evaluate his needs, help him to plan treatment, and carry it out.

Who Is Most Qualified to Diagnose and Treat?

The only professionals who can legally dispense medication for the treatment of psychiatric illness are doctors of medicine and doctors of osteopathy (M.D.s and D.O.s). The therapists best qualified to provide all of these services are psychiatrists with adequate training in biological psychiatry.

All psychiatrists are physicians who have attended four years of medical school and have had at least a year of postgraduate general medical experience plus three years of special training in psychiatry. After a certain number of years in practice, a psychiatrist is eligible to take special examinations, "board examinations" in neurology and psychiatry, the passing of which entitles him or her to use the title "board-certified." Recertification at fixed intervals would be a useful method of ensuring that doctors stay abreast of medical progress. All psychiatrists, like all other physicians, must continue to attend courses and engage in other academic activities in order to maintain their *medical* licenses.

Among psychiatrists, the best qualified to treat depression are those who specialize in the diagnosis and drug treatment of depression, manic-depression, and other biologically caused psychological difficulties. No formal training programs in biological psychiatry exist. Psychiatrists master the field as part of their general psychiatric training or on their own, following their formal training. Until the past 20 years most training programs in psychiatry emphasized the psychological causes and treatment of psychiatric problems (and these programs were often indistinguishable from those given in social work, clinical psychology, etc.). Thus, older psychiatrists generally have *not* had formal training in biological psychiatry. A substantial number have completely retrained themselves, but many have not. This is particularly true among the group of psychiatrists most firmly committed to the psychological treatment of psychiatric problems, such as the psychoanalysts. Many psychoanalysts, despite their training as physicians, are actively opposed to the use of medication as the primary treatment of psychiatric problems.

Many nonpsychiatrist physicians (e.g., internists, family practitioners, neurologists) have also begun to treat large numbers of depressed patients. There are several reasons for this. Often depressed patients who have been referred to psychiatrists will not go, believing that psychiatrists treat only crazy people. They think that accepting such a referral will mean that they are much sicker than they had realized, and they believe that going to see a general physician instead will demonstrate their lack of serious mental illness.

Sometimes a general physician will treat depressed patients, either because there are no competent psychiatrists with biological training in the community or because he has no confidence in the available psychiatrists who specialize in psychotherapy. However, for many general physicians, training in the diagnosis and treatment of depression has been only "on the job." Others, particularly family practitioners, may have had a relatively brief period (three to six months) of training in psychiatry during their post-medical school training (residency).

As we pointed out earlier, general physicians vary tremendously in their skill in handling differential diagnosis, drug management, and psychological assistance for depression. Some deal with most routine cases with great ease and are quick to refer nonroutine cases to biologically skilled psychiatrists. Others do not recognize the possible complexity of depressive illness, approach all kinds of depression in the same way, and provide inadequate treatment. A further problem is that the internist or family practitioner may settle for a partial improvement, although more vigorous treatment or alternative medication might produce complete relief of the depressive illness. He may then refer the partially improved patient to a psychotherapist, who assumes that the remaining problems are psychological. However, because the physician providing the medication may not have provided optimal medical treatment, the remaining difficulties may not be psychological problems at all but biological symptoms that did not yield to the inadequate medical management.

If the patient with a mood disorder does not know how to contact a psychiatrist, he can begin by seeing his family practitioner or internist. He should ask his doctor if he treats mood disorders or refers people with such problems to a psychiatrist. If the doctor prefers to treat depression himself, the patient may decide to remain with him. If the depression does not resolve completely after two trials of medication, the patient should request a referral to an appropriate psychiatrist. For related disorders—manic-depression, panic attacks, atypical depression—the patient should consult a specialist directly.

Nonphysician therapists, such as psychologists, social workers, and pastoral counselors, are handicapped in treating depressive patients because of their lack of medical training.

Although many have doctoral degrees and postgraduate training, their education largely focuses on psychological and social factors in mental disorders. Minimal attention is given to the all-important biological factors. Social workers usually have several years of postcollege education, nurses two to four years of post-high school education that includes varying emphases of the treatment of other medical and surgical problems, and psychologists several years of postcollege training in diagnosing and treating patients. Psychologists are often still taught to use diagnostic techniques that are no longer considered useful by biological psychiatrists, and they were not trained to recognize biological factors in mood disorders and other psychiatric illnesses. As we have emphasized, although nonphysician therapists can play a useful role in the treatment of depression, we do not believe they should be consulted first. In too many instances they may be insufficiently aware of the superiority of medication to psychotherapy in the treatment of biological depression, and they may fail to make a proper referral.

If the patient contacts a "counseling service" or "mental health center," she must be careful that she is not evaluated only by a nonpsychiatrist. Some such services and clinics still operate on the basis that all professionals are equally qualified to diagnose depression. Unfortunately, this is not true, since many are untrained in diagnosis and cannot make the appropriate (necessary) referral to psychiatrists. If the patient is first seen by a such a "therapist," she should request a referral to a psychiatrist, and if this is not made, seek help elsewhere. Otherwise, she may receive inappropriate and ineffective "treatment," may suffer continuing symptoms, and may never be referred to a psychiatrist for diagnosis.

A situation that occurs increasingly often as nonphysician therapists do learn about biological factors is the referral of a patient by such a therapist to a physician or psychiatrist for "medical management" of depression or another psychiatric disorder. In a referral of this kind the physician regulates the medication while the therapist treats the patient with psychotherapy. A possible difficulty with this arrangement is that many of the "psychological" problems the psychotherapist is treating may be additional symptoms of only partially treated biological depression. If so, the monitoring physician may not see the patient frequently enough to provide the best psychopharmacological treatment. If the patient is referred by a therapist, some managed-care organizations will authorize only a one-hour evaluation (for diagnosis and initiation of treatment) and ten to fifteen minute follow-up visits.

Here is an example of a possible misunderstanding of this kind. As we mentioned in discussing possible causes of depression, psychoanalytic theory holds that depression results from anger that is held in rather than directed at the person or situation provoking it. Thus, a psychotherapist might guess that a depressed wife was not expressing her anger at her husband's neglect because she unconsciously thought that expression of anger would lead to his departure—a situation she feared more than his transgressions. In such a case, psychotherapy would be directed largely at "getting the anger out"—helping the wife to express it. One could then have a situation in which a depressed patient was receiving inadequate antidepressant drug management while the psychotherapist's maneuvers were possibly making her worse. Since excessive anger and irritability can sometimes be a manifestation of depression, encouraging the patient to express such emotions might lead to further distancing from the patient's family or other close ones. On the other hand, if the patient was unable to express supposedly repressed anger (which may not be there), she might see herself as a "bad patient," lowering further her already low self-esteem.

The possibility of such treatment mismanagement in psychotherapy is what leads us to emphasize that a depressed patient's treatment should be directed by a knowledgeable physician. If a psychotherapist is necessary, the physician can select one who has learned to distinguish between the psychological symptoms produced by biological depression, the psychological consequences of a biological depression, and other psychological problems that the patient may have. Correctly directed collaborative treatment plays an essential role in dealing with the nonbiological problems that biological depression produces and with the other psychological problems that patients may have simply because they are human.

Finding a Psychiatrist with
Training in Biological Disorders

A logical way to begin looking for a biologically trained psychiatrist is to request a referral from one's family physician. If the physician has not had much professional contact with psychiatrists in the community, one can inquire of the state or district branch of the American Psychiatric Association (APA). The branch will give the inquirer the names of several psychiatrists practicing in the community. The names are usually given on a rotation basis, and the caller can ask whether the psychiatrist is board-certified or not. However, the APA or district branch will provide no evaluation of the psychiatrist's skill, areas of specialization, or interest and training in biological psychiatry.

Another especially good way to locate specialists in the biological treatment of depression is to find out if any nearby university medical schools have a research or treatment clinic for depression (or "mood disorders" or "affective disorders"). Such clinics generally not only conduct research but evaluate new drugs and train young psychiatrists in the diagnosis and treatment of depressive illness. The level of expertise in these clinics is usually high, and they are often able to recommend not only their own staff but psychiatrists practicing in the community.

If the university medical school does not have such a clinic, it is sometimes helpful to ask whether any of the senior staff or members of the Department of Psychiatry see private patients. However, physicians associated with medical schools are not necessarily better trained than physicians in the community. The odds are greater that a physician chosen at random is well trained if associated with a medical school, but some senior physicians at medical schools still emphasize the psychological approach to psychiatric problems. We wish to emphasize that there are many excellent, biologically skilled psychiatrists in the community who are not associated with medical schools. We refer patients to such psychiatrists all the time; some of them are in private practice and some are in good private clinics that specialize in depression.

Many communities have community mental-health clinics, which are supported by federal and state funding and that offer psychiatric services on a sliding-fee scale. The philosophies of the clinics and the expertise of their psychiatric staffs vary considerably. In very many, evaluation is done by non-psychiatrists. In others, all evaluations are done or reviewed by psychiatrists. Community health clinics have the advantage of lower fees, but the prospective patient must ask the same questions of them that she would of any private psychiatrist.

In addition to these avenues for getting help, several national organizations provide assistance.

The Depression and Bipolar Support Alliance consists of patients and families who try to educate the public about depression and bipolar disorder and to help prospective patients obtain adequate therapeutic help. The central branch responds to requests for help by referrals to convenient local branches that maintain lists of physicians whom their members have found helpful. It does not attempt to certify the excellence of the doctors; however, the association's recommendations, based on experience, are very useful. (Address: 730 N. Franklin Street, Suite 501, Chicago, IL 60610. Telephone: 800-826-3632.)

Meeting with the Psychiatrist
for the First Time

In the first interview, which will probably take an hour or two, the prospective patient should ask the psychiatrist about his or her approach to therapy. In particular, it is vitally important to find out what the doctor's policy is regarding the use of medication. An open-minded psychiatrist will not think that such questions are presumptuous and will not conclude that the patient is resisting recognition of possible psychological problems. If the psychiatrist does seem to resent such inquiries, we recommend that the patient seek another psychiatrist.

Before being seen in psychiatric consultation, the patient should prepare a detailed list of all treatments, including medications of any sort, that he has received for any medical or psychological conditions. The actual dates and dosages of medications are crucial for evaluating past treatment. Memory is unreliable with regard to such information. The patient should check with his physician or pharmacist to get the exact names, dates, and amounts.

Depending on the severity of the depression, the psychiatrist may see the patient initially twice a week for two or three weeks, then once a week for a few weeks, and at decreasing intervals thereafter. Psychotherapy is not a necessary component of the initial treatment of biological depression, but the patient and doctor may wish to discuss it. The patient should be sure to raise any questions he may have about his type of mood disorder.

At the outset it is also desirable to discuss openly how the progress of the therapy will be evaluated. An increasing number of psychiatrists now find this approach acceptable, some even draw up contracts with their patients specifying the duties of both participants, the frequency of the meetings, and the point at which progress will be evaluated in order to determine whether the treatment should continue.

Second Opinions

How long should one stay in treatment that is not helping? Over 80 percent of patients with a mood disorder will respond to at least one of three drugs, if each is tried in adequate dosage for a minimum of six weeks. The degree of response may vary considerably. Some patients will experience complete relief of symptoms, others will have some decrease in symptoms, and about 20 percent of properly diagnosed and properly treated patients will fail to respond.

As explained previously, all patients should have an adequate medical examination prior to embarking on a course of medication. If medication has failed to be effective, there should be an even more intensive medical review. In particular, the physician will want to determine if the patient has a mild degree of hypothyroidism. Among its many functions, thyroid hormone affects not only metabolism but also the way the brain functions. Borderline underactivity of the thyroid gland can be detected only by special medical tests. These tests have demonstrated that, in many instances, a lack of response to standard antidepressant treatments is due to hypothyroidism. Often the addition of thyroid hormone "potentiates" the antidepressant and relieves the depression.

If a patient has received three trials of medicine of six weeks each and does not feel any better, she and her psychiatrist should discuss obtaining a second opinion. If progress is not apparent, or if in open discussion the psychiatrist acknowledges uncertainty, it is perfectly appropriate for a patient to request a second opinion, a consultation. This does not necessarily reflect on the competence of the psychiatrist. It is merely a recognition of the fact that no physician can know everything and that some patients' problems can be exceedingly perplexing.

The preceding discussion has assumed that initial treatment has been by a biologically trained psychiatrist. If a patient with the symptoms of unipolar depression (loss of pleasure, loss of interest, loss of energy, etc.) has been in psychotherapy for over three months with a nonbiological psychiatrist or a nonpsychiatrist and has not responded, he or she should obtain a consultation from a psychiatrist who offers biological treatment. Even if the symptoms are unclear and the therapist cannot be certain that the patient is depressed, such a consultation is advisable. Any patient with manic symptoms should consult with a biologically trained psychiatrist immediately.

Recently, the United States Department of Health and Human Services has released an excellent document, titled "Clinical Practice Guidelines" for the treatment of depression. It states, with regard to psychotherapy, that "If there is no symptom improvement at all within 6 weeks, the choice of treatment modality should be reevaluated. For patients who improve but who are still symptomatic after 12 weeks, treatment with medication is a strong consideration."

Some patients with depression, like some patients with hypertension, are extremely difficult to treat. With these patients, even a skilled physician may have to try several medicines singly and in combination before he finds a recipe that works for a given patient. It is hard for a patient to distinguish between a good physician who is systematically trying medicines and a poorly educated one who may be prescribing in a nonsystematic way. However, whenever the patient has doubts about a treatment to which he is not responding, it is sensible to request a second opinion.

Psychotherapy for the Depressed Patient

When a patient who is receiving adequate and successful medical treatment for depression still has several psychological difficulties (demoralization, various day-to-day problems consistent with life circumstances, learned maladaptations), it would be best if the patient's psychiatrist could also handle the psychological requirements. However, adequate training in both the biological and the psychological aspects of psychiatric illnesses is uncommon, which makes finding well-rounded therapists difficult for patients and for referring physicians and agencies. We ourselves, when asked to refer a patient for treatment in a distant city, often must ponder long and hard in order to locate appropriate psychiatrists. We do not have too much difficulty in locating a physician for a patient with a clear-cut biological depression or a reputable psychotherapist for someone with personal limitations or maladaptations that are clearly psychological in origin. But when the patient's problems are a variable mixture requiring careful biological and psychological evaluation, finding an appropriate physician can be very hard.

We would like to emphasize that, in such instances, biologically trained psychiatrists often turn to the many well-trained nonmedical psychotherapists, recommending psychologists, social workers, or others who are equipped to carry out the necessary psychotherapy for depressive patients. Sometimes psychiatrists also recognize that patient support groups, religious groups, and social organizations can provide the necessary support for patients with depression who have special psychological needs.

Conclusion

In closing, we would like to offer one last piece of advice to the depressed patient receiving therapy, who is like any other medical patient receiving therapy. It was advice—a "law"—dispensed by one of the grand old men of American internal medicine to his medical students and interns: "If what you're doing is working, don't stop; if what you're doing isn't working, try something else." Profound wisdom, simply stated.

As scientists and clinicians, we are appalled because depression and manic-depression affect so many people. Even when treated, they are too frequently inadequately treated. This allows unnecessary pain, impairment and, tragically, too many deaths. As working clinicians, we are frequently heartened by our ability to radically improve the lot of confused and suffering people. As scientists, we have shown that our treatments are real, effective, and not simply wishful thinking.

The stigma of mental illness has interfered with proper, humane, and rational care of emotional disorders. This has been confounded by the discrimination against mental illness carried out by funding agencies, in the form of both private insurance and underfunded public mental-health organizations. Proper attention to clinical depression will lower medical costs, increase productivity, and provide solace to the many suffering from depression.

We hope this book will help individuals with undiagnosed depression and manic-depression to recognize their illnesses, to understand them somewhat better, and to seek and receive appropriate treatment.

Epilogue

What Don't We Know?
What's Blocking Progress? What to Do?

WE HAVE BEEN scientists and psychiatrists for over 50 years, and in that time much medical progress has taken place. But what we have learned is that chance observations often lead to clinical breakthroughs that can only be recognized by the prepared mind of a clinician—what is known as "serendipity." That many of the major advances in psychiatric medication have been serendipitous comes as a surprise to even well-informed people. Frequently, psychiatric medications produce unanticipated benefits that don't fit current theories or clinical expectations. These remarkable benefits were responsible for changing our diagnostic system and allowing improved, more specific medications to be prescribed.

Over five decades we have studied emotionally ill people and their treatment. Paul did pioneering, creative studies in the vastly unpopular area of medication for children, wrote the first book on ADHD (attention-deficit hyperactivity disorder) in children, was the first to diagnose ADHD in adults, and demonstrated the effectiveness of stimulant treatment; and Don found a remarkable benefit from using the first widely used antidepressant, imipramine, on spontaneous panic attacks, which led to the concept of panic disorder, as well as proving the value of the concept of atypical depression.

Our point in bringing up our research history is to underscore that these and other therapeutic advances came directly from detailed long-term studies of sick people, whose various treatments sometimes worked and sometimes made matters worse. Unfortunately, current psychiatric research programs have turned away from this fruitful clinical approach to discovering new treatments to focus almost exclusively on basic laboratory studies. But these types of studies still have only a tenuous relationship to either psychiatric illness or treatment because sick patients are not their focus. There is no question that basic studies are important, but their payoff is far from immediate. Our concern is that the federal granting agencies (particularly, the National Institute of Mental Health) and university researchers have effectively abandoned clinical studies of psychiatric medicines to the pharmaceutical industry. We will review this unfortunate shift and suggest remedies.

Recent Progress

The past ten years, since this book's first edition, has seen remarkable, positive, changes in the public understanding of clinical depression. A number of books, written for patients and families, deal with mental illnesses, in particular, depression. These books have been written by professional writers as well as by sufferers from depression. The National Institute of Mental Health has ongoing public-education programs. Public figures, notably Mike Wallace and Senator Chiles, have spoken out about their illness, helping to destigmatize depression and mental illness in general.

Patient support organizations broadened their agenda to support private psychiatric research foundations. These support groups try to correct society's views of mental illness as a mere lack of will power, obtain parity on medical insurance, stimulate research, and promote professional education.

Negative Trends

Despite these advances, negative trends have emerged. The public spends billions on herbal "alternative" remedies and "natural" substances in the belief that they are safer and more effective than the high-tech medicines purveyed by the pharmaceutical industry. This is fueled by suspicion of the industry's profit-driven motive, a distrust of technology, and a romantic return to the good old days, when natural foods and remedies were at hand—unfortunately, a nostalgic, unrealistic view of the past experience with mental illness.

A movement for "animal rights" has ruthlessly exploited a good-hearted, sympathetic devotion to pets, rather than the more sensible concern for animal welfare, both human and non-human.

To counter the stigmatizing beliefs that psychiatric illnesses were psychological in nature, or "psychogenic," the term "brain disease" is now being used as a slogan—clearly more correct than blaming bad mothering or offering other psychological theories to explain biological problems. Unfortunately, HMOs justify swift, inaccurate diagnosis and treatment based on a superficial examination and have relied on this slogan. The influence of HMOs on medical practice cuts patient contact time short, while paying less for care of mental illness. This is a disincentive for skilled effort.

Surveys show that primary-care physicians regularly miss clinical depression. When recognized, it is treated poorly. To do a proper job of diagnosis and care takes time. This is undercut by the current rates set for coverage of mental illness. Attempts to achieve parity for mental illness insurance has, once again, been defeated (2004).

The Continuing Lack of a
Knowledge Base for Medical Practice

Pharmacological treatment is the center of medical practice. When illness drives you to a doctor, you expect medical science to provide an exact diagnosis and to receive a beneficial drug prescription. But when medication is prescribed, just what does the doctor know?

Here are some practical questions for which we do not yet
have definitive answers:

- Patients often have many symptoms and impairments, or
  even several illnesses, both medical problems and a psy-
  chiatric illness. Which symptoms and impairments are
  most or least likely to benefit from this treatment?
- Which drug is best?
- Which drug causes the least side effects?
- What is usually the most effective minimum dose?
- What is the maximum dose beyond which continuing to
  push the dose yields no benefit?
- How fast should the doses be increased?
- How often should medication be given? Will once a day
  work well?
- Which side effects indicate that treatment should be
  stopped?
- How often should the patient be seen or talked with?
- Does the drug affect mental acuity, emotional responsive-
  ness, creativity, sexuality, and other activities? If not now,
  maybe later?
- When will benefit appear?
- How long do you wait before deciding this treatment will
  not work?
- If the first treatment fails, what next?
- What if that fails?
- Does drug withdrawal cause problems?
- Will the drug be affected by other drugs?
- How does this treatment compare to other treatments,
  with regard to benefit, speed of action, side effects, rela-
  tive cost, and chances of relapse?
- Should treatments be combined? Which ones?

We could go on, but the message is plain. These questions
rarely have factual answers. Only a small part of psychiatric
practice is based on hard evidence. The FDA only insists that a
marketed drug outperform placebo and is safe during the short
term, but that is almost all that is known when the drug is marketed and usually well after.

Laws and regulations decide who can market a product, or where houses can be built, or assure safety in industry, or decrease pollution, and so forth. These public actions have enormous, obvious, economic impacts and stir heated arguments.

However, as Marcia Angell, M.D., past editor of the prestigious *New England Journal of Medicine*, states, "The American public seems to be extraordinarily attuned to threats to their health. Issues such as asbestos, the possible cancer-causing effects of birth control pills, the multiple plagues supposedly produced by breast implants, the issue of drug recall by the FDA, the safety of a new vaccination, caused endless discussion, multiple newspaper headlines, hearings in Congress and not infrequently billion-dollar class-action suits."

Yet the sins of taking no action also gravely impact our lives, but these pass unnoticed. A bad drug or a useless diagnostic procedure produces a smaller effect on medical care than our sparse knowledge of effective practice. The questions far outnumber the answers.

These deficiencies are not limited to psychiatry but are evident across all of medicine and surgery. There is a new slogan—"evidence-based medicine"—which urges doctors to use tested and proven treatments. This seems sensible, and is a step in the right direction, but the underlying problem still exists. There are many important clinical questions without evidence based answers. And there is no financial, academic, or political incentive to produce evidence that would answer these questions. Demanding the knowledge required to improve care is not a public demand—although it should be.

Drug Discovery

In psychiatry we are far from knowing the "pathologic mechanism," the underlying biological cause, of many mental illnesses. So our working models of schizophrenia, bipolar disorder, major depressive disorder, panic disorder, obsessive-compulsive disorder, and the like, are incomplete. And yet many claim that basic research will produce quick therapeutic benefits and is required for progress. For instance, the Federation of American Societies for Experimental Biology (FASEB) released a report titled "Federal Funding for Biomedical and Related Life Sciences Research FY 2000 Recommendation." Although FASEB's recommendations are largely sensible, their understanding of clinical research is that it "applies the understanding gained from basic research to problems of human health." For psychiatry this is premature, because of our insufficient knowledge of how the brain works and why it goes awry.

Even for general medicine, the case for the progression from basic scientific knowledge to clinical usefulness is not direct. To use just one example, the recognition of Viagra's erectile benefit was a serendipitous observation made during the investigation of Viagra as a possible anti-hypertensive drug. Patients reported the peculiar "side effect" of enhanced erections.

Once the clinical discovery is made, basic research is required to understand how it works. The problematic reality remains that every major psychotropic drug discovery has been due to clinical observations of unexpected benefits. So an exclusive focus on basic science, in the hope of new treatments, is misguided.

The Process of FDA Medication Review: The Lack of Postmarketing Surveillance

Since the activities of the Food and Drug Administration (FDA) are often misunderstood, we briefly describe how it works. Many people think the job of the FDA is to promote the public health by bringing out new beneficial drugs. But their job is actually to prevent the release of unsafe or ineffective drugs. They are a regulatory agency, whose job is to appropriately say "No"; it is not their job to find or promote useful treatments.

The law says that medications must be proved safe and effective before marketing is allowed. This has led to our current system of FDA drug approval (note this law does not apply to psychotherapy or surgery). After a medication has gone through animal studies for safety and possible usefulness, there follows human safety studies, usually in healthy subjects but sometimes, as with anticancer drugs, in patients. This is referred to as Phase I.

This is followed by openly treating patients so as to observe possible treatment benefits (Phase II). If Phase II is promising, elaborate, usually multisite, double-blind, placebo-controlled, randomized studies of thousands of patients are done (Phase III). Phase III makes sure that early promising effects are actually real.

Once completed, reams of research data are shipped to the FDA for a detailed review that may go on for years. Finally, the FDA may agree that the material is valid enough to be presented to an Advisory Committee. The independent experts on this committee review the various summaries and debate whether the drug is safe and effective, and therefore "approvable," or requires more work, or should be rejected. Their decision is not binding on the FDA.

However, even if the FDA accepts approvability, 10 to 15 years after the first human use, it is still not ready for marketing. The problem is writing the "package insert," which accompanies every bottle of medication and sets the limits for advertising. Its language will enter the ubiquitous *PDR* (*Physicians' Desk Reference*) as warnings, contraindications, and side effects. The package insert must be negotiated between the FDA and the company. This directly affects profitability.

A concerned FDA may demand an insert, rimmed by a black box, in which warnings are highlighted. Such a black box is considered a sales killer by industry. Such discussions usually last months. The company may actually discard a drug as probably unprofitable if a "black box" is required.

The FDA can influence medical caution before marketing. But once a drug is marketed, there is no standard system for postmarketing surveillance—that is, finding out how those who receive the drug are benefited or harmed. Doctors are not obliged to report possible side effects to the FDA, although some do. But even if they do, there is no system to find out if the symptoms that occur after taking a medication are actually due to the medication, or to an interaction with another drug, or to an illness that has nothing to do with the medication, or maybe to unusual allergies of a patient, or something they ate, and so on. Therefore, this unsystematic information about postmarketing side effects includes a flood of misinformation; all added to the package insert, thus protecting the company from suits claiming patients were not informed of possible risks. However, this drastically reduces the worth of the *PDR* warnings, while they scare the hell out of patients.

On occasion, rare dangerous effects such as liver failure or blood abnormalities are reported. The FDA, or the company, may then decide to withdraw the drug from the market immediately. This judgment is usually hasty and political. The pharmaceutical industry is an easy target for accusations of negligence and profiteering. And the FDA is damned if it does and damned if it doesn't: that is, for releasing dangerous drugs into the market but also for taking too long to release promising drugs. Thus, the FDA leans over backward to avoid approving any possibly dangerous drug, which slows down the release of all drugs, but also has a hair-trigger response leading to drug withdrawal. The pharmaceutical industry, spooked by class-action suits, such as the one that bankrupted the asbestos industry, often withdraws products even before the FDA demands it.

This is not a rational system. A proper system of computerized postmarketing surveillance through prescription registrations and symptomatic reporting would let scientific monitors know how many patients are exposed to particular medications, if the side-effect rates differ from the usual, and determine the kind of patient who is at risk for severe side effects. This would be a complicated, difficult undertaking. For instance, it will be hard to tell if a drug given to very sick people is helping or harming. Nonetheless, it is a feasible goal. But nobody lobbies for it.

Some drugs have occasional serious side effects, but are still uniquely useful. For instance, clozapine is an invaluable antipsychotic that can work when no other drug does. However, on rare occasions, it can cause a blood disease that can be fatal. Thus, the FDA required a weekly blood test that markedly decreases this risk. Since no other drug approaches clozapine for effectiveness in difficult cases and since chronic schizophrenia is so serious, the FDA allows marketing, but requires the systematic blood testing.

A similar program could have been developed for nomifensine (considered a uniquely valuable antidepressant) which also can cause a blood disorder. However, given the availability of other antidepressants, coupled with a lack of concern for the subgroup of patients who need that particular drug, no attempt was made to keep this valuable drug available through proper monitoring. The company withdrew it, and it is no longer available.

Pharmaceutical companies are reluctant to search for evidence that a particular drug works best for a subgroup of patients, such as those with treatment-resistant depression. If there are no specific indications declaring when an agent is useful, a "broad" spectrum of action can be claimed. For those who respond poorly to an initial treatment, finding out whether one drug works better than another is important, but again, avoided by the pharmaceutical industry, perhaps in fear of discovering that their drug is worse than the competition. Thus, competitive economic forces within the industry are strong incentives to avoid developing such clinically vital information.

The Special Case of Children and Adolescents

Before marketing, the FDA must approve a medication's safety and efficacy for a particular disorder. However, it is a matter of medical judgment whether a marketed drug should also be used for similar conditions. This is referred to as "off-label" prescribing and is very common.

Children and adolescent depression have not been studied extensively. Therefore, SSRI antidepressants shown useful in adults have been prescribed for children.

To date, only Prozac has been shown safe and effective in child and adolescent depression. There has been much concern that some firms have evidence that their drugs are actually ineffective but have not made this known.

There is even more concern that these drugs may actually cause suicidal attempts, although no actual suicides have occurred in the treatment studies.

This is a difficult situation, since it is not clear, as yet, whether the reported negative effects are due to the drug or to the illness itself.

Therefore, caution dictates that the use of antidepressants in children be restricted to those where medication is clearly needed.

What constitutes a serious depression? A child or adolescent is seriously depressed when he or she has multiple severe symptoms of depression, is seriously impaired in functioning, expresses thoughts such as the lack of meaning or purpose in life, or talks about death or suicide. Serious impairment in functioning refers to a marked loss of interest in activities the youth previously enjoyed, withdrawal from friends and family, and deterioration of performance in school. Because self-harm is a serious risk and because antidepressants may decrease the risk of suicide, the cautious use of the most effective treatment available is one in which the benefits exceed the risks.

Also, any treatment for such children (not just by drugs but also by psychotherapy) requires vigilant monitoring of the child's condition. Weekly reviews are often necessary. It is bad treatment to diagnose depression, prescribe medication, and schedule the patient to be seen in a month. Parents must be educated *that if things do not go well* the doctor must be quickly informed.

Fostering Serendipity

How can serendipitous observations of unexpected clinical benefits be fostered? An environment in which patients are well known to their doctors and easily observed for a substantial time makes the detection of unexpected benefits much more likely. By studying chronically hospitalized patients, antipsychotics, antidepressants, and antipanic agents were discovered. However, in the subtler, inherently fluctuating disorders that are common in outpatients, observing possible benefits is much less reliable. Reports of improvement may be misleading since the improvement may have occurred in spite of the treatment. For instance, sexual inhibition is often caused by selective serotonin reuptake inhibitors (SSRIs). This common effect was not initially noted by industry. After it was clinically obvious, many anecdotes of supposedly beneficial antidotes have been reported. Nonetheless, to this day, no large-scale case series or controlled treatment study has examined how to counteract this important, treatment-impairing side effect. Perhaps the pharmaceutical industry avoids such studies because this openly admits the real importance of this side effect, leading to negative repercussions on marketing and profit. There are few academic rewards for doing such studies. Therefore, our ignorance persists.

The Current State of Psychiatry

An unblinking look at the state of psychiatry must recognize the problematic facts. Psychiatric diagnosis is still at a descriptive level because objective, specific, diagnostic tests have not been discovered. Therefore, similar conditions that actually have different causes and treatment responses are lumped together.

Theories about the causes of psychiatric illnesses are poorly supported and have a bad historical record. Few have survived rigorous tests. The conventional wisdom about how both the psychotherapies and the pharmacotherapies work is superficial. Therefore, attempting to deduce from theories how to improve treatment usually doesn't work.

Research has demolished some simplistic notions, but this has not translated into treatments. The hopes that genetic research will allow laboratory diagnoses of psychiatric diseases have floundered amid the complexity of genetic findings that reveal just how much we don't know. Even though the exact simple genetic mechanism for Huntington's disease was isolated over 15 years ago, and although the damaged protein produced by this defective gene is known, translation into a therapeutic intervention has not yet occurred. This is probably because of the complex, and still largely unknown, cascade of events that take place between gene, gene product, and clinical manifestations in the body and brain. This remains one of the few cases, however, where diagnosis has been made objective, through the use of genetic screening.

Because the major treatment advances in psychiatry have been serendipitous, one would think our scientific leadership would focus on developing clinical contexts that foster serendipity. But this is not the case. "Chance and the prepared mind" require the clinical opportunity for discovery, but the contact of experienced clinicians with possible new drugs is steadily shrinking.

The Need to Focus on Illness

If we really understood normal psychological and brain functions, then understanding psychiatric illness might be straightforward. Attempting to evaluate and treat things that have gone wrong, without first understanding normal functioning seems misguided.

However, the human organism, and particularly the brain, is fantastically complex. The past half century has given us a mind-boggling glimpse of the complexities that remain to be discovered. Every day a new discovery reveals just how much we still need to understand.

Fortunately, medical advances have not depended on first correctly understanding normal functioning, but rather focused on treating illness. Treatments that somehow succeed, highlight what went wrong. This allows the discovery of further treatments that somehow repair or compensate for the still poorly understood dysfunctions.

In medicine, until very recently, the sciences benefited from clinical discoveries rather than the other way around. The development of vaccines and antibiotics fostered the field of immunology. The treatment of scurvy, pellagra, and beriberi led to the discovery of the vitamins that played a role in these diseases, which in turn taught us how the enzymes, the basic biological catalysts, worked. The development of antipsychotics, antidepressants, and anti-anxiety drugs fostered the neurosciences, which may eventually in turn discover the underlying cause of mental illnesses.

It follows that in psychiatry, given our inadequate grasp of what goes wrong and why, that a major research focus should be the detailed, imaginative study of novel therapies on difficult-to-treat illnesses. Focusing on the processes that underlie effective treatments of psychiatric illness suggests testable hypotheses about what went wrong. That is a good bet for advancing both basic knowledge of disease mechanisms and clinically useful understanding. Can we once again focus on the impact of psychiatric treatment and the observation of surprising clinical benefits? This requires radical changes in both drug development and clinical care. It will not happen unless the public, sparked by patient support groups, demand it.

Treatment-Resistant Depression

Carrying out treatment studies in the usual community clinic is simply too difficult. Clinicians object to patients being randomly assigned to treatments because they believe they already know what should be done. Scientifically untrained personnel yield unreliable, misleading measurements. Yet one must evaluate and provide improved treatment for patients with difficult, complicated illnesses. The hope was that the discovery of potent new medications, combined with randomized, placebo-controlled, double-blind trials, would create evidence-based comparisons of different treatments. This has not occurred. If the first treatment fails, hardly anything is known about what the second treatment should be.

One solution would be to develop standing, research-oriented clinics and day hospitals to provide systematic collection of data.

Absence of Sound Psychotherapy Research

There is no industry, comparable to the pharmaceutical industry, to support the study of psychotherapy. The American Psychological Association (which used to be research focused) has turned into a psychotherapists' guild. However, they also actively lobby for the right to prescribe medications, with a recent success in New Mexico. This organization's domination by privately practicing psychotherapists, who claim promising results for many of their therapies, reached the point that many scientist members split off to form the American Psychological Society in 1988. However, this new group does not focus on evaluation of treatment.

Studies of psychotherapy benefits rarely take into consideration the effects of suggestion, family support, or the passage of time. Comparisons of different psychotherapies that supposedly work by entirely different mechanisms rarely show one more effective than another.

Competing claims about the relative value of pharmacotherapy and psychotherapy, with regard to cost, speed of onset of effect, acceptability, degree of benefit, ability to maintain effects over time, and so forth, are almost never based on actual collaborative trials between experts with differing backgrounds. The rare collaborative expert comparative trial is almost never repeated. Nonetheless, the popular press often seizes on surprising, undocumented claims for psychotherapeutic benefit.

Public Pressure

The general public thinks it knows too little to even express an opinion about the goals and methods of medical research. But it was public pressure, sparked by the philanthropist Mary Lasker and the psychopharmacologist Nathan Kline, that led Congress to force the National Institute of Mental Health (over the objections of its director) to develop the Psychopharmacology Research Service. A system for funding independent academic clinical psychopharmacological studies was thus started. Unfortunately, this effort lapsed when NIMH effectively abdicated support of such clinical studies to the pharmaceutical industry.

Patients can affect government and industry policies, if they clearly understand what will benefit them and are well organized. The well-organized, public relations savvy success of the AIDS activists and the National Organization of Rare Diseases convinced Congress that federal incentives should spur treatment development for their constituencies. Realistically improving medical practice will also require political organization and public pressure.

Development of a Proactive Federal Medical Practice Improvement Agency

There is no federal agency primarily charged with improving the public health by developing medications or monitoring practice. The FDA is regulatory, not proactive. Their job is to say, "No," not to search for opportunities to say, "Yes." The National Institute of Health primarily supports research in the basic sciences rather than treatment and practice issues.

A National Board of Medical Experts should be part of a proactive agency. Pharmacological experts would review undeveloped opportunities, including medications studied abroad. Potentially useful drugs with expired patents provide no financial incentive for companies to invest in establishing new uses (e.g., lithium as an add-on for refractory depression). Therefore, this federal agency should offer the cheap financial incentive of increasing the period of marketing exclusivity, if the potentially useful drugs are found to satisfy FDA requirements for safety and efficacy. Other incentives are needed for promising compounds "sitting on the shelf" because they are thought to be unprofitable. The same applies to likely new uses for marketed drugs that the drug industry does not pursue because of insufficient projected profitability.

In all these cases there is no actual increased federal expenditure on research. Rather, industry is given new incentives, if they accomplish specific goals that public health experts agree are worthwhile.

This new proactive agency should develop joint NIMH/industry/FDA collaborative programs on clinical trial methods. The precedent for such cooperation comes from the development of drugs that requires improvement in assessment methods (e.g., Alzheimer's disease and obsessive-compulsive disorder).

The largest sets of data relevant to improving clinical trials are owned by industry and protected by law, even if used to gain FDA approval. For regulatory approval, the pharmaceutical industry naturally presents the most favorable analyses. They rarely make raw data available to independent researchers; therefore, potentially informative independent analyses cannot be done. There is almost no opportunity to independently compare drugs, except through weak techniques applied to data summaries.

We believe that the data files that support all the analyses published in medical studies should be made available, on publication, by placing the underlying data on the Web. After all, publication of data summaries affirms that the supporting data is real and correctly analyzed. Independent, critical reanalysis would amplify peer review. The current peer review system does not require, or even allow, the reanalysis of primary data. Financial incentives for investigators and journals to carry out such analyses should be provided by the proactive agency.

Also, nobody is under any obligation to publish a study saying that a drug is useless. This can be very valuable knowledge but can also be against the economic interest of the sponsors. There is a peculiar ethical problem here. Patients volunteer to undergo the risks and discomforts of a clinical trial, so as to increase medical knowledge. Shouldn't informed consent include the fact that they may be wasting their time or shouldn't the Institutional Review Boards require that the sponsor guarantee that detailed publication will be forthcoming? Such ethical issues are largely ignored.

Clinical Research Centers

This new Federal Medical Practice Improvement Agency could establish a network of Clinical Treatment Research Centers of excellence. These centers would supervise multisite, research-oriented, model clinics and day hospitals, whose job would be to expertly evaluate patients who have not responded to usual clinical care. Careful, reliably documented studies of treatment processes and outcomes can develop outcome norms for these groups, defined by diagnosis, economic status, treatment history, and comorbidity.

All research is, to some degree, a gamble on an unknown future. Treating and studying many well-delineated patients, some who may also have medical, psychiatric, and substance-abuse conditions, would define expectable treatment outcomes. Therefore, if a new approach looks better than expected, this provides a rational basis for undertaking the expenses and difficulties of a proper clinical trial.

Public Involvement

A regular public conference program on medication development should be started. Our society has made only piecemeal adjustments to the flood of extraordinary pharmacological advances. Given recent developments in molecular and genetic biology, enormous strides are possible. However, without a well-formulated, continued national discussion and debate concerning how to foster and regulate these advances, the current period of public misinformation and regulatory chaos will get even worse. The current debate over whether estrogens should be used for menopausal symptoms is a forerunner of even more heated arguments.

Developing a proactive program for drug development and monitoring is essential. Many of our suggestions are controversial. Some may be wrong. Our intention is to stimulate open discussions of thorny issues by informing the public how they are being short-changed with regard to achievable medical advances. The democratic political process has a chance to work constructively only if correct information is available and debated.

Index